W9-BWH-749

DISCARD

HOW TO BE BLACK

HOW TO BE BLACK

BARATUNDE THURSTON

HARPER

An Imprint of HarperCollins*Publishers*
www.harpercollins.com

HarperCollins books may be purchased for educational, business, or sales promotional use. For information, please write: Special Markets Department, HarperCollins Publishers, 10 East 53rd Street, New York, NY 10022.

Get exclusive extra content, join a community, and expand your blackness at http://howto beblack.me/bought. You can also find us at facebook.com/howtobeblack and on Twitter with the hashtag #HowToBeBlack.

All illustrations are courtesy of the author.

FIRST EDITION

Designed by Lisa Stokes

Library of Congress Cataloging-in-Publication Data has been applied for.

ISBN: 978-0-06-200321-8

12 13 14 15 16 ov/rrd   10 9 8 7 6 5 4 3

To my mother, Arnita Lorraine Thurston, who embodied authenticity and taught me how to be black, American, human, and awesome. I miss you, Mommy Lady.

Contents

HOW TO BE BLACK

Thanks for Celebrating Black History Month by Acquiring This Book

Be not afraid of blackness. Some are born black. Some achieve blackness, and others have blackness thrust upon them.

—Shakespeare[*]

WELCOME TO *How to Be Black,* a book I hope will serve as a thrust of blackness in your general direction.

First, let's get the disclaimer out of the way. This book is not *How to Become a Black Person If You Are Not Already Black.* You cannot use this book as a magic potion. You cannot digest the printed copy and expect some supernatural physical transformation beyond painful indigestion. If you purchased the book with the intention of changing your race, I thank you for your money, but there will be no refunds. None.

---

[*] William Shakespeare never wrote this, but wouldn't it be great if he had? Come on, you know it would! Black Shakespeare! Yay!

Now, more to the heart of the matter, the odds are high that you acquired this book during the nationally sanctioned season for purchasing black cultural objects, also known as Black History Month. That's part of the reason I chose February as the publication date. If you're like most people, you buy one piece of black culture per year during this month, and I'm banking on this book jumping out at you from the bookshelf or screen. Even if you're reading the book years after its original publication, it's probably February-ish on your calendar. That's absolutely fine. You're doing your part to celebrate blackness, whether you are black or not, so I'm going to run with that and offer you some helpful instructions for how to take further advantage of this month. You asked for it. You got a book called *How to Be Black*, so don't start complaining now.

There are, of course, small everyday opportunities to celebrate blackness: covertly swapping birthday confetti to red, black, and green colors; giving the secret head nod and mild fist pump to a black person across the restaurant; stealthily assembling forty-acre tracts of suburban land and mules for conversion into African-American farmland and militia-training grounds. The list is endless. But what should one do during the official month designated by the U.S. government for the celebration of black history?

Even for black people, this is no simple task, and if you're not black, well, wow, the confusion! One can find oneself at wits' end in an attempt to properly recognize the contributions of an entire race to an entire nation across an entire month. Things weren't always this complicated.

In 1926, Negro History Week was established by the black historian and author Carter G. Woodson. It was expanded to a full month in 1976 after the government realized that black people's demands for self-determination and an equal seat at the table of American opportunity could be satisfied either through a comprehensive program of economic and political empowerment or by extending the buying season for postage stamps featuring noteworthy black Americans by a factor of four.

Since the establishment of Black History Month, other groups have been similarly honored.

- **March** is shared between Women and Irish-Americans, and **May** among Jews, Asian Pacific-Americans, and "older" Americans. Old people get one-third of a month!

- **June** has been reserved for honoring gay and lesbian pride along with Caribbean-American heritage, explaining June's better-known name as Best Parades Ever Month.

- Given the rapid demographic changes facing America, you would expect a Latino History Month by now, but National Hispanic Heritage Month covers **September 15–October 15**. While it is a four-week period of time, it's not technically a "month" and forces those honoring the nation's Latinos to buy two calendars.

- **November** is National American Indian Heritage Month, in which Americans are encouraged to recognize the contributions of native peoples to our great nation by eating turkey and enjoying the bounty of the stolen lands beneath our feet.

For schoolchildren, the Black History Month ritual is simple and automatic: make posters out of construction paper; attend the obligatory assembly; and learn one Negro spiritual. Exactly one. Probably "Wade in the Water."*

The options for adults, however, extend far beyond this narrow set of preprogrammed activities. In order to simplify your celebratory options, I've hand-selected this list of ten ways one can celebrate the contributions of African-Americans† to these United States, carefully designed with the non-black person in mind. At the end of the list, I provide a tool for you to assess your celebratory skills, so pay close attention.

1. CHANGE THE WALLPAPER ON YOUR COMPUTER OR MOBILE PHONE TO AN IMAGE OF A SLAVE PLANTATION

We'll start with something simple. When your friends or coworkers ask you why you have a picture on your screen of slaves working the fields, you should smugly reply, "I believe in honoring the people who made America possible, don't you?" Then gently touch your screen in a longing fashion and shake your head slowly. Just be sure to avoid saying anything like, "I know slavery was a horrible institution, but—" This sentence is impossible to complete in any reasonable way regardless of whether or not it is Black History Month and is especially troublesome on the presidential campaign trail. (I'm looking at you, Michele Bachmann.)

---

* It's also possible that you will sing the Black National Anthem, "Lift Every Voice and Sing."
† Throughout this book I will use the terms African-American, black, and Negro interchangeably. There is rarely a logic to it, so please try not to overthink it.

2. WATCH BET

Never mind that it's not owned by a black person anymore. You can still learn a lot from BET. Primarily, you will learn that black people love reruns, and if you're lucky, you'll catch the Tyler Perry movie! I know the Internet Movie Database says Perry has written over ten films, and there may be several titles and even different casts, but if you've seen one Tyler Perry movie, you've experienced the entire canon. The man has only made one film, and you can catch it on BET, repeatedly.

3. AVOID BEING EXPLICITLY RACIST

This one can be a struggle for many. Racism is everywhere, and it comes naturally. But it's considered to be *extra* offensive if you are explicitly racist toward black people during Black History Month. If nothing else, it shows a lack of discipline. If you're serious about hating black people, prove it by delaying that hate for a few weeks. Racism is exhausting, and you could use a break. Take one! On March 1, you'll return to peak form, fired up and ready to marginalize.

4. KNOW THE KEY PEOPLE

There have been lots of unsung heroes in the history of Africans in America, but they're unsung for a reason. To appear knowledgeable, you need to know only a few: Dr. Martin Luther King Jr., Rosa Parks, Malcolm X, Harriet Tubman, Sojourner Truth, Jackie Robinson, Muhammad Ali, W. E. B. Du Bois, Booker T. Washington, J.J. from *Good Times*, Frederick Douglass, Langston Hughes, Thurgood Marshall, Dr. Martin Luther King Jr., and Barack Obama. When in doubt, see if there's ever been a feature-length film about the person or a T-shirt sold using his or her image. If the answer to both of these questions is no, move on.

5. OBSERVE ANYTHING AND EVERYTHING THAT PRESIDENT OBAMA DOES

Every single thing Barack Obama does is historic. If he clogs the toilet in the White House bathroom, he's the first black president to damage White House plumbing. If he forgets the words to the "Star-Spangled Banner," he's the first black president to do so. If he continues to wage a war in Afghanistan, bails out Wall Street to avert financial disaster, and continues several of his predecessor's anti–civil liberties practices, he's the first black president to let down his progressive base. Regardless, it's all wonderfully historic and beautifully black. By observing the nation's first black president, you are indeed, directly and quite literally, observing black history! If someone asks how you're celebrating Black History Month, it is perfectly acceptable to say, "Oh, I'm following President Obama on Twitter. I like my black history in 140 characters or less."

6. HUM A NEGRO SPIRITUAL

Spirituals are very important to black people, for we can be a soulful and musical people (which you would know if you watched BET, as instructed earlier). If you've never heard a spiritual, don't let that stop you. Just start humming and hold the note. Then occasionally change the note. Add a little vibrato. Then return to the original note. Shake your head back and forth for emphasis. Get extra points for doing this while waiting for the office copy machine to finish a job, and get double extra bonus points for doing it when a black employee can see and hear you. (For a better understanding of this, spend extra time in the chapter "How to Be a Black Employee.")

7. READ *THE AUTOBIOGRAPHY OF MALCOLM X*

Better yet, just watch the movie, starring National Black Friend Denzel Washington. I especially love the part where he organizes the Fruit of Islam to protest outside of the Harlem police station, then surprises his mother by purchasing a mansion for her in the country with all the drug money he made being a rogue cop with Ethan Hawke in Los Angeles, all while coaching a debate team at a historically black college. Most of what you need to know about black history can be gleaned from these scenes.

8. ACQUIRE A NEW BLACK FRIEND

Denzel and I are busy men. We can't be the black friends for all of non–Black America. So it would behoove those of you who are not black to get your own. If you find yourself in the unfortunate position of being black-friendless, you can either go to the nearest black church and strike up a conversation, or just fire up Facebook, search for "black people," and start clicking "Add Friend" on the names in the resulting lists. Technology is amazing and quite a time-saver.

9. PUT PICTURES OF BLACK PEOPLE ON YOUR (NON-FACEBOOK) WALL

Anyone who's seen Spike Lee's *Do the Right Thing* knows that if there's one way to activate the dormant riot gene in an African-American, it's by failing to place images of their peers on the walls of a neighborhood retail establishment, especially a pizza shop. To keep your shop glass intact, and to avoid unnecessary aggravation and insurance hassles, just put some pictures of jazz and blues musicians on the wall. If people ask, just say it's Muddy Waters.

10. DEMONSTRATE YOUR SUPERIOR KNOWLEDGE OF BLACK HISTORY IN FRONT OF YOUR BLACK FRIEND(S)

This is an advanced-level activity. If you have had no prior experience with black people—the black friends newly acquired this month do not count—I strongly urge you to forgo this action. Neither Baratunde Thurston, HarperCollins, nor any representatives thereof can assume responsibility for you if you choose to ignore this warning. For those of you who have black friends already, good job! February is a good time to show how committed you are to understanding your friend's struggle. As much as possible, ask your friend about his or her opinions on some extraordinarily specific detail related to black history and culture.* This is not the time for generalities. Get down in the weeds!

For example:

"Have you heard the latest tracks from the Carolina Chocolate Drops? It's like this amazing fusion of old-school jug band meets Gaelic music meets hip-hop. Oh, you haven't heard of them? Man, you should really check it out! It's so real!"

Your black friend will absolutely appreciate your knowing more than him or her about some aspect of black culture. You will be living proof of the value of Black History Month! Carter G. Woodson would be proud.

---

* It is perfectly acceptable and even encouraged for you to use this book as an example.

While active observance of Black History Month is its own reward, there are more tangible benefits for those who exuberantly celebrate this month. Below, you will find a box detailing the different levels of recognition and privileges associated with your efforts.

Number of Activities:
0–1

Award Level:
Honorary KKK Member

Award Detail:
Really? Over the course of twenty-eight to twenty-nine days, you couldn't manage to complete more than one activity? That's essentially a hate crime. Please, try harder next year. I mean, how hard is it to visit BarackObama.com and do *one* other thing? You get no extra privileges.

Number of Activities:
2–4:

Award Level:
Tolerator of Black People

Award Detail:
Not bad! While not overexerting yourself, you managed to exceed the minimum. You can use this award to eat lunch at the black table in your school or office cafeteria without receiving any funny looks from black people. If someone seated at the table responds to you in an unwelcome manner,

just show them your Tolerator Level award and your copy of this book. They will understand. This offer is only good for one-time use and expires within forty-three minutes of activation.

Number of Activities:
5–9

Award Level:
Negro Lover

Award Detail:
Well, well, well! It looks like somebody really loves black people. Go ahead with your bad self. You get *three* black-table lunches for use within a year; early access to any new albums by the Roots for life; and twice a year for the next five years, the ability to call out black people who you think are being overly sensitive about race.

Number of Activities:
10

Award Level:
Official Friend of Black America

Award Detail:
By completing all ten items, you have proven your commitment to the black American community far above and beyond what is necessary. In addition to all the benefits associated with the lower-level awards, you also have earned the right to attend two Secret Black Meetings a year, the unconditional for-giveness of one racist outburst, and a reusable tote bag.

And that's how you celebrate Black History Month. If you only acquired* this book to check off your Black History Month obligations, I suppose you could stop reading now, but you already have the book. You might as well keep going, because there's a lot more to being black than February.

THIS IS A BOOK about the *ideas* of blackness, how those ideas are changing, and how they differ from the popular ideas promoted in mainstream media and often in the black community itself.

You're probably familiar with the popular concept of blackness: hip-hop, crime and prison, fatherless homes, high blood pressure, school dropouts, drugs, athleticism, musical talent, *The Wire*, affirmative action, poverty, diabetes, the Civil Rights Movement, and, recently, the U.S. presidency. Some of these concepts are stereotypes. Some are true. Most are negative. But in the age of President Barack Obama, all of them are limiting and simply inadequate to the task of capturing the reality of blackness. The ideas of blackness that make it into mainstream thought exclude too much of the full range of who black people are. Whether it's musical taste, dancing proficiency, occupation, or intellectual interest, all nuance is ignored for a simpler, often more sellable blackness. In this book, I will attempt to re-complicate blackness, exposing the challenges, the fun, and the future of being black

---

* I often say "acquired" instead of "purchased" when referencing your relationship with this book. I'm just acknowledging the reality. Illegal Internet file sharing of copyrighted works of literature about the black experience is destroying the publishing industry and demands government action. Please write your member of Congress before it's too late.

in the United States. It's also a convenient way to make you care about my life story.

My name is Baratunde Thurston, and I've been black for over thirty years.

I was born in 1977 in Washington, DC, in the wake of civil rights, Black Power, and *Sanford & Son*. My mother was a pro-black, Pan-African, tofu-eating hippie who had me memorizing the countries of Africa and reading about apartheid before my tenth birthday. My Nigerian name was not handed down to me from any known lineage, but rather claimed and bestowed upon me by parents, who demanded a connection, any connection at all, to Mother Africa.

Yes, I grew up in the "inner city," at 1522 Newton Street, and I survived DC's Drug Wars. Yes, my father was absent—he was shot to death in those same Drug Wars. But it's also true that I graduated from Sidwell Friends School, the educational home of Chelsea Clinton and the Obama girls, and Harvard University. I love classical music, computers, and camping. I've gone clubbing with the president of Georgia, *the country*, twice.

My version of being black adheres as much to the stereotypes as it dramatically breaks from them, and that's probably true for most of you reading this—if not about blackness itself, then about something else related to your identity. Through my stories, I hope to expose you to another side of the black experience while offering practical comedic advice based on my own painful lessons learned. For example:

In "How to Be The Black Friend," I shine a light on the type of black person who quietly does as much to promote positive interracial relations as any prominent civil rights activist ever could. In my opinion, The Black Friend is a national hero and should be honored for exemplary service.

In "How to Speak for All Black People," I give you the low-down on how to break into the exploding world of black pundit-ocracy on cable news. There is always some black-related thing happening somewhere in the world, and journalism can't fill all those television programming hours, so those cameras might as well be pointed at you!

"How to Be The Black Employee" prepares you for life as one of the few minorities in an office setting, reminding you that you actually have *two* jobs—the one on your business card and being black—and offers key dos and don'ts for the all-important office holiday party. Here's a hint: dancing is involved.

Other chapters include "How to Be The Angry Negro" (because sometimes it's necessary) and "How to Be The (Next) Black President"—it could be you!

But wait, there's more!

The idea of a book that claims to cover "how to be black" is, of course, preposterous, but I'm doing it anyway, and I'm not alone. Because the topic is so large and because my experiences can't comprehensively represent those of millions of people, I recruited a few other voices to help this book live up to its title.

I interviewed friends and colleagues I felt were strong new models of "how to be black." These are seven people who do blackness well, and together they form The Black Panel I call upon throughout the book to weigh in on important issues.

Cheryl Contee is the cofounder, with me, of the blog *Jack & Jill Politics* and a partner at Fission Strategy, where she specializes in helping nonprofit organizations and foundations use social media to create social good.

damali ayo is a conceptual artist, author, and comedian. She created Rent-A-Negro.com in 2003 and is the author of *How to Rent a Negro* and *Obamistan! Land Without Racism*. She is also the creator of the participatory performance piece *National Day of Panhandling for Reparations*.

Jacquetta Szathmari is a comedian and writer and creator of the one-woman show *That's Funny. You Didn't Sound Black on the Phone*. She's also a Libertarian.

Elon James White is a comedian and creator of the Web video series *This Week in Blackness* and the Web radio show *Blacking It Up*.

W. Kamau Bell is a comedian and creator of the one-man show *The W. Kamau Bell Curve: Ending Racism in About an Hour*. He offers a two-for-one ticket deal to those who bring someone of a different race to the show.

Derrick Ashong is a musician, entrepreneur, and television host. He cofounded the band Soulfège and hosts *The Stream* on Al Jazeera English. He was raised in Ghana, Qatar, Brooklyn, and suburban New Jersey.

Christian Lander is the author of *Stuff White People Like*. He isn't black. I had to include one white person to defend against the inevitable lawsuits claiming reverse discrimination, and also to establish a control group.

As you can see, this is a rock-star panel. To its members, I posed questions such as "When did you first realize you were black?" "How's Post-racial America working out?" and "Can you swim?"

They have done more than provide color commentary for this book. They have helped me find the heart of it.

In the final chapter, "The Future of Blackness," I combine my own conclusions with those of the people I interviewed and humbly lay out a complete Grand Unified Theory of Blackness with a vision for a people and a nation. I did not set out to do this, but it happened, and it's kind of awesome.

If you are black, many of these stories and lessons and hopes will ring true to you. Maybe you prevented a race riot in your school by employing diplomatic back-channels to ease tensions between black and white students. Maybe you renounced your blackness for a few hours after being told by other black people that the thing you do so well makes you not black. Maybe your coworkers think you've just *got to* have an opinion on every single move President Barack Obama makes. This book is yours.

If you're not black, there is probably even more to be gained from the words that follow. They may help answer the questions you'd rather not ask aloud or they may introduce a concept you never considered.* You will get an insider perspective, not only on

---

* For example, one of the chapters in this book contains a detailed plan for the implementation of white slavery. Can you find it?

"how to be black" but also on "how to be American," and, most important, how to be yourself. This book is yours as well.

Finally, just in case you were wondering, no black people were harmed in the making of this book.

Yours in blackness,
Baratunde Rafiq Thurston

@baratunde on Twitter. And the book's hashtag is #HowToBeBlack

Where Did You Get That Name?

BARRY. **BARRINGTON.** Baracuda. Bartuna. Bartender. Bartunda. Bartholomew. Bart. Baritone. Baritone Dave. Baranthunde. Bar— Brad.

This is a representative sample of the world's attempts to say or re-create my name. For the record, it's Baratunde (baa-ruh-TOON-day).

I've trained for decades in the art of patiently waiting for people to butcher my name. It's often a teacher or customer service official who has to read aloud from a list. I listen to them breeze through Daniel and Jennifer and even Dwayne, but inevitably, there's a break in their rhythm. "James! Carrie! Karima! Stephanie! Kevin!" Pause. "Bar—" Pause. They look around the room and then look back at their list. Their confidence falters. The declarative tone applied to the names before mine gives way to a weak, interrogative stumbling:

Barry? Barrington? Baracuda? Bartuna? Bartender? Bartunda? Bartholomew? Bart? Baritone? Baritone Dave? Baran-thunde? Bar—? Brad!!

The person who called me Brad was engaged in the most lazy and hilarious form of wishful thinking, but all the others kind of, sort of, maybe make some sense. This experience is so common in my life that I now entirely look forward to it. Like a child on Christmas morning who hasn't yet been told that Santa is a creation of consumer culture maintained by society to extend the myth of "economic growth," I eagerly await the gift of any new variation the next person will invent. Can I get a Beelze-bub? Who will see a Q where none exists? How about some numbers or special characters? Can I get a hyphen, underscore, forward slash? Only after letting the awkward process run its public course do I step forward, volunteering myself as the bearer of the unpronounceable label and correct them: "That's me. It's Baratunde."

I LOVE MY NAME. I love people's attempts to say it. I love that everyone, especially white people, wants to know what it means. So here's the answer:

My full name is Baratunde Rafiq Thurston. It's got a nice flow. It's global. I like to joke that "Baratunde" is a Nigerian name that means "one with no nickname," "Rafiq" is Arabic for "really, no nickname," and "Thurston" is a British name that means "property of Massa Thurston."

In truth, Baratunde is derived from the very common Yor-ubwa Nigerian name "Babatunde." A literal translation comes out something like "grandfather returns" but is often interpreted as

"one who is chosen."* Rafiq is Arabic for "friend or companion."
And Thurston, well, that really probably is the name of the white
guy who owned my people back in the day.

Of all the groups of people who react to my name, I've found
that white people are the most curious about its meaning and origin. Upon hearing of its origin, they want to know when I last
visited Nigeria. Other non-black people are nearly as curious,
assuming "Baratunde" to be a family name that goes back generations, that was passed to me through a series of meticulously
traceable biblical begats. Black Americans, on the other hand,
rarely even pause to ponder my name. Considering how inventive
black Americans have been with their own names, that's not very
surprising.

Where I never expected any particular reaction, however, was
from Nigerians themselves. Nigerians have very strong opinions
about my name. They don't like it, and they want me to know.
Constantly.

I call this phenomenon the Nigerian Name Backlash. Rarely
does a week go by without a Nigerian somewhere on the Internet finding and interrogating me. I first encountered the NNB
when I was twelve years old. I called my Nigerian friend, who
went by "Tunde," on the phone, but he wasn't home. Instead,
his *extremely* Nigerian father answered, and our interaction pro-
ceeded as follows:

"Hello, who is calling?"

---

* Note: "One who is chosen" is not the same as "the chosen one." The latter has a lot
more pressure associated with it and generally ends badly for the namee. I have no
religions established in my memory, yet.

"Hi, sir, this is Baratunde."

"Where did you get that name!?"

Let's pause the exchange right here, because you need more context. Father Nigeria did not simply ask where I got the name as one might ask, "Oh, where did you get those shoes? They're really nice. They're so nice that I need to know where you got them so I can possibly get myself a pair." No, that was not the tone. The tone was more along the lines of "Who the hell do you think you are coming into my house, stealing my gold, priceless family jewels, my dead grandmother's skeleton, my porridge, and attempting to walk out through the front door as if I would not notice? By all rights, I should kill you where you stand, you thieving, backstabbing boy."

Shocked by the question, but determined to be both honest and respectful, I answered.

"I got it from my parents," I told him.*

"Do you even know what it means?" Father Nigeria asked me in the same way you might ask a dog, "What model iPad do you want?" Fortunately, I knew exactly what it meant, and I proudly answered, "It means grandfather returns or one who is chosen."

He reacted swiftly and loudly. "No! It means grandfather returns or one who is chosen."

As I was about to explain to him that I'd just said the very same thing, he launched into a tirade: "This is the problem with you so-called African-Americans. You have no history, no cul-

---

* After years of comprehensive anthropological study, my team of researchers found that most children acquire their names from their parental units.

ture, no roots. You think you can wear a dashiki, steal an African name, and become African? You cannot!"

Remember, when this self-appointed Father Nigeria decided to indict, judge, and reject all of African America for its attempts to rebuild some small part of the ancestral bridges burned by America's peculiar institution, I was twelve years old and not in the best position to argue that maybe he should calm down and stop acting like a bully.

His reaction stunned me, but it also prepared me for the regular onslaught from members of the Nigerian Name Backlash community. While he made a sweeping dis against all black Americans who sought cultural identification with Africa, most other Nigerians I've encountered have more technical complaints. Every few weeks a new batch finds me on the Internet, usually Twitter, and swarms with the same basic set of questions and challenges:

"Are you Nigerian?" they excitedly ask.

"No. My parents just wanted me to have an African name."

"You know your name is Nigerian, right?"

"Yes."

"But it is wrong, your name. What is this 'Baratunde'? You mean '*Baba*tunde,' right?"

"No."

"Where did you get that name?"

Sigh.

My name has served as a perfect window through which to examine my experience of blackness. For non-blacks, it marks me as absolutely, positively black. However, most of the vocal Nigerians I've met (which is to say, most of the Nigerians I've met) use my name to remind me that I'm not *that* black.

When Did You First Realize You Were Black?

FOR AMERICANS, some days are unforgettable: the day JFK was assassinated, the day Osama bin Laden was killed, the day Flavor Flav's Fried Chicken restaurant went out of business. For many black Americans, a similarly unforgettable experience takes place the day you realize you're black, and if it's not a moment of black self-awareness, it's probably—nevertheless—the moment you were introduced to the idea of black as something negative.

I recall three moments of black self-awareness.

The first moment occurred in kindergarten.

My mother worked in Washington, DC's, L'Enfant Plaza at the Office of the Comptroller of the Currency.* Across the street, the Department of Housing and Urban Development ran

---

* OCC is an independent bureau within the U.S. Treasury Department. Its mission is, primarily, to regulate national banks. My mother was a computer programmer at OCC, writing and inspecting code in the COBOL programming language, because, you know, single black mothers love programming, son!

a kindergarten in its child-care center. The HUD building has a distinctive design: a curved concrete structure in the shape of an elongated X with evenly spaced, recessed windows arrayed in a precise grid. When seen in conjunction with the storm trooper outpost–looking parking attendant booth, it felt as if we were on the set of *Star Wars*. Tucked away at an interior corner of a courtyard was the child-care center's playground. That's where I developed a crush on a little girl in my class (insofar as a four- or five-year-old even knows what that means).

I would demonstrate this by throwing things at her and singing Paul McCartney and Stevie Wonder's "Ebony and Ivory" in her general direction. She was white.

I don't remember anyone making a big deal of our racial differences, but I remember noticing them myself. Also, I sang "Ebony and Ivory" at her, which I still can't believe. The next year, she and I had moved on to different worlds, and I became obsessed with the song "Uptown Girl" by Billy Joel. Not until writing this book did I realize how perfect for the situation the lyrics of that song are. Essentially, she was living in her "whitebread world" and I was her "downtown man." Could you imagine a more perfect metaphor? I don't think so.

The second moment of black self-awareness came courtesy of my mother and her sense of interior design. Our household was stocked with images of proud blackness: a Malcolm X portrait, stacks of jazz, soul, funk, and R&B records, and two massive paintings, one integrating a set of ankhs* and the other of a Black

---

* The ankh is an Egyptian hieroglyph symbolizing the key of life or eternal life. It appears often in Egyptian art, Egyptian tombs, and season five of *Lost*.

Power fist. It's hard not to know you're black when you're physically surrounded by it on a daily basis.

This painting loomed over me on the walls of my early childhood home.

The third moment of awareness occurred on a childhood camping trip with my mother and my friend Reginald somewhere in Virginia, I think. Reggie and I were playing alone in the nearby lake when a little white boy approached us from the shore and loudly announced, "There's niggers in the water! Look at the niggers!" I like to imagine that our first reaction was to spin around, searching and frantically yelling, "Where!? Niggers? Let me at 'em! Where are they?"

Reggie and I had a hard choice to make in that moment. The reason we knew each other is that we were in karate classes together back in DC, and we were very good at karate. We conferred on whether or not to use our combined karate skills to kick this little racist's ass, but considering our location in the Who-Knows-Where Woods of Probably, Virginia, we decided against it. In that moment, the black pride I absorbed in my home was balanced by the embarrassment, rage, paranoia, and self-restraint that often accompany blackness in the outside world of America.

Most black people have their own coming-of-blackness story, and in the process of putting this book together, I conducted interviews with several friends and professional colleagues I thought could lend an alternate, and often more eloquent, voice to the questions raised by *How to Be Black*. Here are the members of The Black Panel recalling their first realizations of being black or what blackness meant.

W. KAMAU BELL

I first realized I was black when I was in first grade at a small, private school in Boston. I was playing doctor with a bunch of kids and this one girl, it was her turn to kiss me, and she didn't, and she ran away laughing, and the other kids ran away laughing. And the thing I realized at that point [was] that I was black and they were all white.

That was the first time I remember feeling like black was somehow separate from the norm. I think I knew I was black before then, because my mom would not have let me not know I was black. There would have been no way that she would have let that information slip. "It's cold outside. Take a jacket. And you're black."

CHERYL CONTEE

I first realized I was black in nursery school, when a little girl told me that I was black. And I told her, "No, I'm beige." I knew what beige was, even though I was four, because I went shopping a lot with my mother and grandmother, and so I knew taupe, beige, and the difference between the two. And I could read, and I knew from crayons, I knew the color beige. I used it a lot to draw myself.

So I was really disturbed, because she held her ground. She was fairly certain that I was black. So I came home, and I remember I couldn't really move past the entrance of the house. And I needed to talk about the fact that this little girl said that I was black, and that I, in fact, found myself to be beige. [My parents] reacted like any black intelligentsia: we went to the library.

I would actually call it a series of seminars for my brother and me, in terms of African-American culture through the ages, going back to Egypt, actually. And I remember the Saturday when we went to the big library in Wheaton. We didn't go there except for special occasions.

ELON JAMES WHITE

I first knew I was black when I was a child and my mother and my uncle yelled at me because I had a broken thought process on race. They were talking about how the cops were dealing with black people, and I started to explain to them that "Maybe if black people stopped committing so many crimes, then the cops would leave them alone," and they stared at me. Then I was like, "Well, I'm a black male, and I haven't been arrested for anything, so obviously it's not just being black."

And then they cried.

DAMALI AYO

My first memory of realizing I was black was told to me by my mom. There's two. I remember being in tap dance class when I was two years old, and apparently I had a concern that the teacher would turn me white. So I was very aware early on that I liked being black and I wanted to stay that way.

And then my mother tells a story about going out to dinner at some point, and our family's out and I'm just a baby. And the waitress, white waitress, comes over and says, "What a cute little baby!" And I just go, "Ahhhh!" So my mother interprets that as a racial tension. I mean, maybe it was her perfume or something. But you know, my mom's read was, "My little daughter knew what was up."

DERRICK ASHONG

I didn't know at first. I was born in Africa, so everybody was black. We don't really think about it like that. Here, everyone's like, "Is he black? Is he white? Is he black?" In Africa, you don't ask. The assumption is that you're black. Therefore, what becomes more important is other things. What your name is, where you come from, what language you speak, what's your culture, what's your tribe, et cetera. So I didn't know I was black.

When I was eight, I moved to the Middle East. I think the Middle East is the first time I discovered I was black, because people

would come up to you, and they'd [say something in Arabic,] which
translated to, "Hey, this is a black guy."

    Then I went to a British school in Doha. British people let
you know you're black. They still were trying to hearken back to
them old days. I'm like, "Dude, we is all free now, we are all free.
You have nothing but this little island and the Falklands. You have
nothing else." But they will remind you.

    I started to understand what it meant to be black insofar as an
American context when I moved back to the States. I did [my last
two years] of high school in suburban New Jersey.

    I'm a city kid. I didn't know what the suburbs was like. I
discovered it was not that nice. That's when I discovered that
apparently being black is not good. Things like, "Black people are
not supposed to be smart." I had no idea. I'm messing around, getting
As. Stupid ass. I thought you were supposed to be good. Little did I
know that I should play more basketball, read less books. But this I
learned when I got back here.

JACQUETTA SZATHMARI

    I think I've always known I was black. I mean I grew up in a
black neighborhood; it was never like a process of discovering I was
black, but I can say I remember [the first time I was] insulted about
being black. That's when I realized that maybe black could suck a
little bit.

    I was doing swimming lessons at 4H camp or a day camp kind of
thing, I was going to go dive in the water, and some white kid made
a comment about grease in my hair and how it was going to ruin the
entire Chesapeake Bay. I was like, "Wow, okay, that's racism, and
that's what it's going to mean for a little while for me to be black."

CHRISTIAN LANDER

My whole life in Toronto, I was very, very aware of being white at a really young age. The [black] experience in Toronto is very different, because of the way immigration patterns worked. So most of our [black] population is actually Afro-Caribbean, people who moved up from Jamaica, Trinidad, Guyana. My understanding for most of my life about black culture was really more Caribbean-based.

I'd say I learned fairly early on from the Toronto experience, and the rest is really the American black experience, which came from media, television, and so forth.

You like how I included a white Canadian? Booyah. Diversity in *How to Be Black*? Check.

Mama Thurston

MY **FAMILY** has been black for a long, long time.

While I have yet to pursue Harvard professor Henry Louis Gates's crime scene–investigating, genealogical origin-hunter project,* I can go back a few generations based on stories my mother shared and documents my sister and I discovered after she passed in 2005.

My great-grandfather was named Benjamin Lonesome, and he was born in 1870 in Caroline County, Virginia. According to my mother, he was part Native American,† born a slave,‡ and taught

---

* Henry Louis Gates is a Harvard University professor and director of the W. E. B. Du Bois Institute for African and African American Research. In 2006 and 2008, he hosted *African American Lives* on PBS and explored the genealogical backgrounds of several prominent black Americans. In 2009, he, President Obama, and a white Cambridge, Massachusetts, police officer shared a beer at the White House.

† I advise you to be suspicious of any black American whose family does *not* claim a blood connection to Native Americans. That's a clear sign of a racial infiltrator who has not done enough research.

‡ If you're paying attention and have a decent knowledge of U.S. history, you'll notice

himself to read. According to his obituary, he moved to Washington, DC, in 1896 and started working for the Highway Division of the DC government in 1900. He died at the age of ninety-six.

Based on the photos I've seen, he was tall, thin, and handsome. My mother held her grandfather in extremely high regard, so much so that I was named in his honor.* Benjamin Lonesome fathered two daughters, one of whom was my maternal grandmother, Lorraine Martin.

I don't have many memories of my grandmother. By the time I came along, she and my mother had an extremely frayed relationship, so I only saw her a few times. What I do remember is that she liked vodka and smelled of cigarettes, and her house had the aroma of their mutual accumulation. What I didn't know until after my mother's passing was that in 1954, my grandmother was hired as "the first colored clerk in the U.S. Supreme Court building," according to the *Washington Afro-American* newspaper. When asked by the paper what she thought of working in the Supreme Court building, my grandmother described it as "sort of awe-inspiring." The woman for whom she worked was a personnel officer named Catherine Waddle. When asked what she thought of my grandmother, Waddle described her as "just fine."

---

that my great-grandfather was born after slavery officially ended. As with many government programs, slavery continued beyond its official end date in many parts of the country.

* My name is derived from the Nigerian name "Babatunde." In the Yoruba language this roughly translates to "the spirit of my mother's grandfather has returned in me." See the chapter "Where Did You Get That Name?" for more on how I ended up with a Nigerian name and no known Nigerian roots.

My grandmother was highly respected in her community, directed the Sunday school choir at her church, and loved to travel. She didn't always love being a parent, though, and took the extraordinary step of sending my eight-year-old mother to an all-black boarding and reform school in Cornwells Heights, Pennsylvania. The Holy Providence School was founded by Katharine Drexel of the Sisters of the Blessed Sacrament, a Catholic religious order created to recruit Native Americans and blacks. Attending the school, though a year behind my mother, was Ed Bradley, who would become one of America's best-known journalists through his work on *60 Minutes*. Within ten years of my mother's time at Holy Providence, basketball legend Kareem Abdul-Jabbar would also attend. I remember my mother talking about her time at this school, but I don't know if she ever realized that some of her schoolmates went on to become some of the most prominent and successful black people in the country.

You don't need to have special qualifications in child psychology to imagine how being shipped off to a Catholic boarding school on the outskirts of Philadelphia would make a little DC girl feel. This letter written by my mother to her own mother captures the reality perfectly:

Dear, Mother
I am having fun but? I do not like it here. I am mad at
you. Please send me some cookies and a Sparkle Plenty doll.
They can have dolls here. Please send it because I do not
have anything to play with.

Yours Truly,
Arnita

But the best part of the letter comes in the form of a note added by someone clearly not my mother. Written in a large, perfect script at the bottom of my mother's note is simply the word "Over," and on the other side of the page in the same script is:

If your little girl is dissatisfied, we'd be glad to have her bed for children who are anxious to come.

Sister

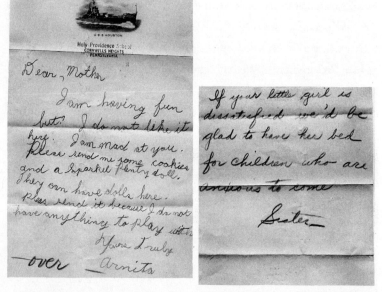

A letter from the very young Arnita Thurston to her mother from boarding school.

Wow. That letter might as well have been signed "Warden." These sisters weren't playing! They got all Patriot Act on a little girl's letter to her mother.

My mom didn't attend Holy Providence for long. After returning to DC, she went to Benjamin Banneker Junior High School and McKinley Technology High School, and for a while seemed to play and dress the part of the appropriate, God-fearing Negro woman my grandmother wanted her to be. I even have a photo of my mother sitting on the National Mall wearing a dress (below the knees) and holding a basket! How quaint. But my mother was also questioning her church's missionary activities to "save the heathens" in Africa, and she began socializing and politicking with blacks from across the Diaspora who lived in DC: Nigerians, Eritreans, Caribbean people, and black American activists.

Soon she was partying with brothers named "El Dorado"— picture a smooth, lanky brother with leather boots, blue-and-white-striped bell-bottoms, polyester dress shirt, and an afro that shone like the sun—and protesting in streets and on radio stations for black liberation. My mother was turning our family even blacker!

Arnita Thurston as Appropriate Negro Woman.

El Dorado aka
The Coolest Dude Ever.

Arnita Thurston (center) as Revolutionary Black Woman.

My sister was born into the eye of the Radical Mama Thurston storm in 1968. She lived her first nine years with my mother in one of many centers of black cultural and political activity: the Envoy Towers apartment building on 16th Street in Northwest DC. My mother partied and played music in clubs and smoked reefer,* and her parenting style could be rough, relying heavily on the same corporal punishment she had received growing up.

I had a slightly different version of Arnita Lorraine Thurston. Shortly before my birth in 1977, my mother found a row house in a listing of estate sales, and she delivered phone books and sold home-cooked dinners to help raise the down payment for my childhood home at 1522 Newton Street. By the time I came

---

* Another word for marijuana!!!!!

along, eighty-one years after my great-grandfather had moved to DC, my mother no longer smoked, had mostly given up physically disciplining her children, and would increasingly become committed to an often-annoying health-food diet.

I recall her many experiments in healthy eating with some pain. We often shopped at a health-food cooperative, purchasing items like rice cakes; Grape-Nuts cereal, which was essentially gravel; and skim milk, which is like a watered-down version of the milk you know and love. I'll never forget waiting at the checkout counter of the Takoma Co-op and seeing "carob-covered" doughnuts, which should have been called "infuriatingly not-chocolate" doughnuts.

On nearly every trip to the co-op, we were the only black people in the market, and when my friends visited our home, they would notice that instead of Cheerios cereal, I had some absurd healthy alternative called Tasteeos. If the cereal were actually tasty, its name would not be Tasteeos. It was embarrassing!

My mother also had a deep affection for the outdoors, and she planned many family activities around long car rides, hiking, biking, and camping. Whoever said black folk don't go camping forgot to tell Arnita Thurston, who thoroughly enjoyed spending a Saturday afternoon tent-shopping at Recreational Equipment International (REI). My mother was constantly organizing field trips for me and my friends: hiking in the Blue Ridge Mountains, biking along the C&O Canal, camping on the Outer Banks of North Carolina. The thing is, it's not like she would just drop us off and tell us to "enjoy the nature." No, she was hiking and biking and camping right alongside us. Her own peers thought she was nuts.

Without spending much of her very limited funds (I wouldn't own a video game console or subscribe to cable television until I graduated college in 1999), my mother concocted activity after activity to engage my mind and body. She enrolled me in the DC Youth Orchestra Program, where I learned to play bass and performed at the Kennedy Center and in Knoxville, Tennessee. She enrolled me in tae kwon do after some kids jumped me and stole my bike. She enlisted (yes, enlisted) me in an all-black Boy Scout troop, the highlight of which wasn't the camping trips but rather the field trip we took to a DC Masonic temple, where we grilled the tour guide on the Masons' liberal use of African symbols, all of which he denied.

Under my mother's tutelage, I was becoming a miniature black activist myself. When I was eight, she gave me a book about apartheid, because, you know, how else am I supposed to learn how the world really works? She made me learn all the countries in Africa and quizzed me on them using a map on the wall of her bedroom. I accompanied her to community organizing meetings and stop-the-violence vigils and black cultural festivals on a regular basis.

My mother's parenting strategy was consciously designed to pass on the lessons she'd learned in her life. For example, unlike her own mother, she encouraged spiritual belief but religious flexibility. When I decided to switch from the Catholic church four blocks away to the Episcopal church across the street merely because it was closer, she was fine with that. She just insisted that I be part of *some* community. The QUESTION AUTHORITY bumper sticker that would grace my lockers and notebooks from seventh through twelfth grade is one she gave me, always reminding me that just because someone has authority over me does not mean they deserve my respect. This was clearly counter to the programming she'd received in her own upbringing, and she was determined to break the cycle.

Otherwise, she simply kept me so busy that I couldn't get involved in the increasingly troublemaking activities outside our front door. As the 1980s progressed, so did the breadth and destructive effect of crack cocaine on Washington, DC. I had seen friends' older siblings go from selling lemonade to selling crack and then watched as many of them were carted off to prison. I witnessed an addict brutally beaten with the stones from our front yard, likely because he couldn't pay. I observed as my mother took hundreds of photographs of drug deals going down across the street, not to turn over to the police but because she sensed the historical significance of this terrible transition. Having preserved most of her collection, I'm glad she documented the environment of my early childhood so comprehensively. I was a little black boy living in a war zone. Our own mayor was a crackhead.

When the HBO show *The Wire* came out, I recognized so much of what was on my television screen from my memories of my own neighborhood. As I've reflected back on both, I realize that my neighborhood was just like *The Wire*. We had the drug dealing, the police brutality, the murders. Well, it was *almost* a perfect match. We had everything *The Wire* had except for universal critical acclaim and the undying love of white people who saw it. Of course, eventually white people would fall in love with my old neighborhood as development and gentrification have led to its supporting a subway station, wine bars, and even a Target. Back in the day, I lived in a black neighborhood under siege. For a single black woman raising a boy, this was a terrifying environment. In a 1992 *Washington Post* series about mothers raising black boys in the inner city, the caption on the photo of my mother and me states:

> *Arnita Thurston says she acted like a crazy woman trying to protect Baratunde from the streets.*

Thanks to my mother, I survived that war. At twelve years old, I was a bass-playing, tofu-eating, weekend-camping, karate-chopping, apartheid-hating, top-grade-getting, generally trouble-avoiding agent of blackness.

How Black Are You?

THIS BOOK was almost called *How Black Are You?*
In the summer of 2009, I bought a bottle of wine in the Park Slope neighborhood in Brooklyn. I didn't know much about wine and still don't, but I didn't want to ask the shop employee and then pretend like I cared about her in-depth description involving earthy hints of nutmeg and subtle karmic rainbows of frankincense or sadness or whatever. Instead of admitting my ignorance and seeking help, I browsed the bottles and waited for a sign.

That's when I spotted the label "Negroamaro." This was the sign! I would buy this bottle because it had the word "Negro" on it. I did not know what "amaro" meant, and I did not care. Clearly, this was a red wine created for a discerning black connoisseur.

Later that week, I got up early to catch a flight, and as I rummaged through the kitchen counter of my friend's apartment, looking for something to eat, I spotted the empty bottle of Negroamaro. I thought, "That's pretty black of you, Baratunde."

As with most of my thoughts, I decided this was something I should share with the Internet, so I fired up the Twitter app on my phone and instigated a battle of blackness with my friend and fellow Brooklyn-based comedian Elon James White.

On Wednesday, July 29, 2009, at 7:32 a.m., I pressed "send" on the following message:

> this weekend i picked my red wine because it was called "Negroamaro." that's how black i am. @elonjames #HowBlackAreYou

Two minutes later, Elon responded, "Challenge, son?" and it was on. For the next several hours, we went back and forth trying to prove our blackness in a game of satirical one-upmanship. Others saw the #HowBlackAreYou hashtag flying across their screens and decided to join in. Before long, thousands of #HowBlackAreYou tweets had been generated.

I later retold this story in a technology conference keynote address called "There's a #Hashtag for That," and got the attention of an editor at HarperCollins. After I met with her and her team, the title "How to Be Black" was born. I thought an entire book on "How Black Are You?" was a bit much. (But "How to Be Black" felt just fine!)

Still, that original question interests me. It is an inextricable fact of blackness that one will at some point be referred to as "too black" or "not black enough" by white people, black people, and others. I've yet to meet the Negro who is "juuuuuust right" to everyone. So I turned the question over to The Black Panel. Here's some of what they had to say in answer to the question "How black are you?"

W. KAMAU BELL

I guess we need to know who's on the scale. I would probably say I'm in the middle. I'd say I'm solidly in the middle. I think I've spent most of my life in the middle of blackness, maybe just north of the middle as I've gotten older. I think I get more reason to be black the older I get.

It's like everything. The older you get, the more you get calcified in whatever direction you were going in. I feel about racism the way a lot of guys feel about male-pattern baldness. "This was supposed to be done by now!" Which makes me more black, like "Okay, then I'm going to really step up my game, my black game."

CHERYL CONTEE

I'm pretty black on the inside. That said, genetically, it's obvious there's a little bit of a mix here. And that's something that I've gotten to know over time more extensively through the oral histories of my family, very quietly learning the large extent to which people actually chose to live in the black community to be with the people that they love, which is really awesome and amazing. So I do pay homage to those other heritages, but I feel very much, very strongly, rooted in African-American culture.

That said, I think that there is a stereotype that you're not really black unless you grew up dodging bullets, or eating food stamps, or . . . I don't know, actually engaging personally in rap battles or break dancing. I didn't do any of those things. I may have witnessed some break dancing and some rap battles. Okay, that may have happened. But I didn't personally do that.

Sorry, eating . . . Did I say that, eating food stamps?

ELON JAMES WHITE

How black am I? It depends on the day of the week. It depends on who you ask. It depends on what situation I'm in. It depends on if my white girlfriend shows up. It depends on what topic happens to pop up.

I'm fairly black to people. I've gotten blacker. Like, I wasn't that black for a while, but then I got really, really black. And apparently when I got really black, it wasn't because I did anything specifically black, like I wasn't all of a sudden rocking hip-hop and wearing a hoodie.

I got black when I was like, "You know what, I see racism in a lot of things that people don't like to acknowledge."

And they're like, "Why are you so black?"

And I was like, "Whoa, but I didn't do . . . It's institutionalized."

"Yes, Negro, we understand you're militant, get over it."

"I haven't even raised my fist. I like brunch! I don't know why you're yelling at me!"

I remember my uncle said that I was trying to be a white boy, because I referred to my mother as "mother." I would go, "But mother is saying so and so." [He would say], "Why you try to talk like a white boy?" That's stupid.

In high school—I must have been in tenth grade—a classmate turned to me:

CLASSMATE: Why do you talk like the teacher?
ELON: What are you talking about?
CLASSMATE: You try to talk like the white kids.
ELON: What white kids? [I went to a black school.]

I found myself constantly defending my place in the ranks of blackness.

DAMALI AYO

I am so black that the other day a black person asked me what race I am. That's how black I am. I was like, "Excuse me?" I apparently am the switchy-changy black person. People like to see me as white or as black as they like to see me. I'm so black that everybody says I look like their cousin. I am so black that I don't have to bring up the race card. I am the race card. I am so black that I grew up with a black history bulletin board in my hallway as a child. I'm so black that my father looks like Malcolm X. That's how black my shit is.

DERRICK ASHONG

I am very black. I come in the more ebony shade of jet! I'm a little chocolate-flavored chocolate.

I remember a kid in high school, who said to me once, "Yo, you're not really black. You don't have any slave blood." And I was like, "Wow, you have not been going to enough school. And we need to stop talking, because I would like to get to college someday."

For me, I'm very Pan-African, I'm very much in touch with my African roots. I speak my father's language. I get by in my momma's language. When I was in college, I did Afro-American studies because I wanted to study African-American culture and see what the differences were.

I was really interested in what happened in the African Diaspora and how you could think about diasporic identities and how having those identities, understandings of each other, could empower and strengthen your understanding of self, rather than feeling like, "You came up from this circumstance, and this is the length and the breadth of your history," which is largely told by someone outside of your community, who may not have the same vested interest in you feeling good about yourself, or seeing the value in who you are and where you come from.

I engaged in that kind of study, and that is where I think a lot of my idea of blackness comes from. And it's an inclusive sense.

In a nutshell, I am black insofar as I embrace the idea of a Pan-African and diasporic identity. But in my language, if you ask me who I am, I'm Ebebinyi. *I'm an African. The word we use for a white person is* Obrunyi, *which is a non-African. The color thing, it does not compute.*

JACQUETTA SZATHMARI

I don't think I'm very black. It's been a point of contention for other black people for a long time. People have always made it very clear to me that I wasn't being black enough. Then I've had lots of white people [say], "I don't even notice you're black!" Which usually means you're not poor and smoking a five-piece on the corner and trying to rob my sister. I don't think I'm considered to be very black in the mainstream sense.

However, [2012 Republican presidential candidate] Herman Cain* makes me a lot blacker. [He] wears a cowboy hat and just

---

* At the time of this book's writing, Herman Cain was a Republican presidential candidate. He is a black man best known for having been the CEO of Godfather's Pizza. I feel quite confident that by the time you read this book, his campaign will only exist in the past tense. If I'm wrong, then it means the country has fallen into ruin more quickly than I could ever have imagined, and there are probably roving bands of feral, armed children dominating the streets, which begs the question, *says ridiculous stuff that most black people wouldn't say. I think characters like that make me blacker by comparison. [There are] shades of blackness, and I think that I was towards the lesser black, but then if you have weird people coming along, then that pushes me towards the center, which is where I like to be.*

I'm also from the country . . . I'm from the Eastern Shore of Maryland, which is a wretched place . . . I always considered that black. Black people are country. That's what I thought until I got older and then I met black people who were like, "No, black people [are] hood." I was like, "Oh, okay. Well, now I can't do that either, because I'm from a cornfield."

When I went to boarding school, I met a lot of African-Americans who were . . . legitimately inner city or playing it up to try to retain some kind of blackness. Their whole thing was about Do the Right Thing, *urban culture, Spike Lee. And I'm like, "This guy just seems angry and disgruntled." That was not my experience of blackness.*

I had never had to fight to make a space for my blackness, because on the Eastern Shore you're black or you're white, but more important, your family's been there for four hundred years, and you're from the Eastern Shore. If you come from another place, even if you're one year old, and you died at one hundred on the Eastern Shore, [they'd say], "Not a local." So it was more about that identity of being from Maryland and being from the Eastern Shore.

I'd never had to prove the blackness thing until I got out and

---

what are you doing reading this book? You should probably be foraging for scrap metal and hoarding ammunition.

older and other black people were like, "Hey, wait a minute. I'm
black, you're not."

No, I didn't ask Christian how black he was, but I did ask him
about how *white* he was:

CHRISTIAN LANDER
  I'm about as white as it gets. My family came over on the
Mayflower and then left the United States to stay loyal to England
and moved to Canada during the Revolutionary War.

As his is the most expert opinion I could find on the subject, I
also asked him about notions of "whiteness," especially since most
of the *Stuff White People Like* checklist is based on beliefs, values,
and tastes, not phenotypical traits.

At my high school, anyone who liked something on the list and
was not white was called white, was accused of acting white.

- *A "coconut" is brown on the outside and white on the*
  inside. You could use that for Indian, you could use that for
  Latino, too. It's your choice of which ethnicity you wish to
  disparage.
- *"Banana" is yellow on the outside, white on the inside,*
  which is for Asians. The Twinkie is another replacement.
- *"Oreo" is obviously black on the outside and white on the*
  inside.
- *I actually would probably be called what is known as an*
  "egg" in my high school, which is white on the outside,

yellow on the inside. I mean, I live in Koreatown, I grew
up in Chinatown.

We have it all. We have a wide variety of food-people: coconut,
banana, Oreo, whatever you want.

My own introduction to food-people, to blackness as a mere
facade for interior whiteness, came with a change of schools.

Do You Know What an Oreo Is?

ACCORDING TO DC's school districts at the time, my graduation from Bancroft Elementary School in the city's Mount Pleasant neighborhood should have been followed by my attendance at Abraham Lincoln Junior High School a few blocks south of our home. There was just one problem with this regulation as far as my mother was concerned: kids at Lincoln got stabbed.

I'm not sure how often child-stabbings occurred at this educational institution, but the fact that Lincoln had such a reputation, coupled with my penchant for getting bored in the classroom due to finishing my work early, led my mother to look for alternate schooling. Because my older sister had attended private or at least specialized schooling (Catholic school, magnet school, and an arts public school) my mother felt that I, too, should have the benefits of a non-public education. Thus began my tour of Washington-area private schools.

The first was Georgetown Day School. All I remember from my visit is making some really shitty pottery in an art class. I'm sure they did other things at that school, like math and English and the scientific method, but I just remember that shitty piece of pottery.

The second school I visited was called Green Acres, and it had three strikes against it.

Strike One: the name. "Green Acres"??? That sounds like a rehab center for matrimonially challenged politicians. That name was just a bit too soft for a black kid from the city. Speaking of soft, my initial interest in the school was based entirely on the crush I had on a girl from my church, never a good reason to make a six-year commitment.

Strike Two: building design. The school had no hallways. I don't mean that the inside of the building consisted of dark matter or "The Nothing" from *The Neverending Story*. I mean the classrooms all had doors to the outside, and kids walked outdoors to get from one class to the next. I later learned that this is a common design in warm places like Southern California and Hawaii, but Green Acres was in Bethesda, Maryland, whose climate offers three full months a year with average low temperatures at or below freezing.

Strike Three: the worst basketball game I've ever seen. The day I visited, Green Acres had a boys' basketball game. I was shocked to find that the boys' team had a girl starting (bravo), and she was the best player (what?), and *Green Acres lost the game 50–2!!* Even though I wasn't a fan of basketball, I refused to go to a school that could get its ass so thoroughly whipped.

With Georgetown Day and Green Acres failing to meet my

standards, the remaining school was Sidwell Friends. The school is now famous for educating Chelsea Clinton (two years behind me) and Malia and Sasha Obama, but when I enrolled, the school's reputation wasn't quite as glamorous.

I arrived a bit of a fish out of water. While I wasn't from the deep hood of Southeast DC, by Sidwell standards I was about as hood as it got at the time. I was pretty black, for a black guy. I arrived suffering from a mild medical condition known as "Ebonics" or "Black English Vernacular." This condition caused me to "axe" people questions and caused the other students to ridicule me. I knew perfectly well how to speak perfectly well, but around friends, I was used to a more relaxed linguistic style. Eventually, my Ebonics went into full remission, and I could be paraded before boards of trustees, donors, and parents with little risk of institutional embarrassment.

Sidwell was such a foreign environment. First, there were just so many white people. They were everywhere! That wasn't normal. My neighborhood and previous school were all black and Latino with the exception of two white students in my grade: a boy and a girl. The boy's name was William. The girl was Willamena. Seriously. As far as I knew, all white people had the same name! But at Sidwell, I met Patricks, Bronwens, Julias, and Phillipas.

My classroom experience was similarly inverted. At Sidwell, usually I was the only black student in the room, and this resulted in me being deputized as some sort of Assistant Professor X whenever anything black were to come up in the curriculum. Reading Harriet Beacher Stowe? Everyone looks at Baratunde. Watching *Eyes on the Prize?* Everyone looks at Baratunde. In science class, learning about Black Lung? Everybody looks at Baratunde. It's as if everyone expected me to carry the knowledge of some sort of Negropedia* filled with answers to all things black for the edification of white classmates.

While the introduction of massive quantities and qualities of whiteness brought landmark changes into my life at Sidwell, the biggest change was probably my discovery of new types of black people.

The school had a buddy program for new students, and I was paired with a black kid who had been at the school his entire life. The name for such students was "lifers," which is very death row–y, which should tell you something. In my first weeks at the school, I remember my buddy pulling me aside with a secretive look in his eye and a hushed tone to his voice. Clearly, serious extracurricular education was about to go down, and I was prepared to soak it up.

"Yo, do you know what an Oreo is?" he asked me.

I paused and stared blankly, thinking, "Of course I do. It's a cream-filled chocolate wafer manufactured by the Nabisco Corporation since 1952, and it's mad tasty." What I actually said was, "You mean like the cookie?"

"No." He shook his head gravely. "An Oreo is somebody who's black on the outside and white on the inside." He then pointed to a student I hadn't yet met and said *that* kid was an Oreo.

I looked across the room and saw a skinny, slightly nerdy black kid hanging out with some white friends, and thought, "Why are

---

* What's that? There *is* a book called *Negropedia*? By Patrice Evans? Is it still February? Let's go buy it right now.

you picking on that kid? Seems to me a perfectly legitimate way to finance an eventual presidential campaign!"

After all, *that* kid's parents were paying good money for Sidwell, and I doubt it was just so *that* kid could socialize with other black kids. White friends cost money! Roughly $30,000 per year plus books.

Wealth-Related Horse Violence

MY FATHER was shot and killed when I was six years old. He was involved in a drug deal gone wrong. He was the buyer. These facts have always annoyed me.

No boy wants his father to die. Being a black boy in Washington, DC, in the 1980s, you especially don't want him to die of drug-related gun violence. It's too stereotypical. The only thing that could make it worse is if he'd not only been attempting to buy drugs but if the deal itself went down inside a KFC restaurant.

This is where the annoyance originates. If he had to die in 1985, why couldn't he have been competing in a Hamptons polo match and gotten trampled by a horse? That would at least give his child a story for the ages.

FRIEND: Hey, Baratunde, how come your dad never comes to your soccer games?
ME: Oh, he normally would be here, but two years ago, he was in the finals of the Mercedes-Benz Polo Challenge when Chad

Worthington III's horse, Barbaro, got out of control. My father was tossed from his own horse, Colonel Tabasco, and crushed. Sadly, he's just another statistic in the epidemic of wealth-related horse violence striking down black men across the country.

Despite having lost my father, I'm not bitter or overly sad about it. I never have been. In part, I was too young to have developed deep bonds with him. On top of that, he didn't live in the house with us, so I wasn't used to seeing him every day. In fact, I only have six memories of him at all.

MEMORY #1: REMOTE-CONTROLLED BOAT

We were visiting someone's house. I don't know whose. I was probably five. Five-year-olds don't care whose house they're in, so long as there are toys to play with. I must have slept there, because my memory is of taking a bath. I don't imagine you just bring your son over to someone's house in the middle of the day and say, "Hey, mind if my kid takes a bath? He really likes to be clean."

So I was in the bath, and my father came in, and he watched as I played with a remote-controlled boat. I've always loved remote-controlled vehicles, but that boat was my favorite.

MEMORY #2: BURRITOTUNDE

My father worked construction. I recall my mother and him waking me up extremely early (pre-sunrise) one day and putting me in the car as we went to his work site. In order to keep me comfortable, allow me to stay asleep, and maximize the cuteness of the scene, they rolled me in a blanket like a burrito.

I love burritos.

MEMORY #3: COUSINS

I've been quite accustomed to having a small family: my mother, my sister, and whatever pets we had at the time. However, my father had a huge family, and I have an unknown number of cousins on his side. One Saturday, we went to the house of one of his relatives, and I was left in a room to play with my cousins.

They were all far older than me, and as such, I was their entertainment system. Small child equals plaything to older children. Their favorite activity was to let me stand up and tell me to walk across the room, but then one of them would grab me from behind by my belt and pull me back down. They did this for a long time, this human yo-yo shtick. My father was nowhere to be found during this torture.

I hate cousins.

MEMORY #4: BEER

I was in my father's pickup truck as he drove somewhere. He had a can of beer open (gateway drug!) and offered me a taste.* It was disgusting, and since then, I've generally found all beer to be disgusting. Over the past decade, I've found three types of beers I actually like:

1. Lindeman's Framboise, which isn't really beer
2. Chocolate stouts (mmmm, chocolate)
3. German Weißbier and its derivatives

---

* Only now, as I'm documenting this memory, has it occurred to me that operating a motor vehicle while drinking beer and offering some to your five- or six-year-old son is one of the worst, and most illegal, parenting decisions a person can make.

I can pretty well tolerate Corona (great commercials) and Heineken (I have positive memories of Amsterdam). All other beer is ass, and I will not put in the work to acquire the taste for things that taste like ass.

MEMORY #5: PRESENTS!

It was Christmas, and my father visited our house and delivered the biggest bag of presents I've ever seen, at least in proportion to my body size. I don't remember any of the gifts. I just remember being blown away by the size of the bag and the number of boxes.

I love presents.

MEMORY #6: DEATH

I don't remember how my mother set it up. We were in the living room, which doubled as my bedroom in our Newton Street house, and the sentence "Your father is dead" fell from her lips. I hesitated briefly, sorting out what this meant. A few beats later I started to cry, but I wasn't crying for the specific man named Arnold Robinson. I was crying over the idea that I was supposed to have a "father" and now my "father" was gone. The idea of losing him is what felt bad.

She gave me a choice as to whether or not I wanted to attend the funeral, and I could see no point in it. Outside of my brief interactions with the torturous cousins, I didn't know anyone on my father's side of the family, and the idea of hanging around a dead body surrounded by crying strangers did not interest me, so I chose not to go.

Some years later, I came across his death certificate in the family file cabinet. Death certificates are remarkably cold, analytical, and frightening accounts of our mortality. I would have understood "he got shot," as that seems like the type of thing capable of killing a person. But the certificate offered extra detail:

> *bullet wound of chest, lungs, spine and spinal cord, followed by paraplegia and bronchopneumonia*

In other words: he got shot.

Why Are You Wearing That White Man Over Your Heart?

Never point a gun at anybody. Never store a gun under your pillow. Treat every gun as if it were loaded. Keep the muzzle pointed in a safe direction. Keep the action open when not in use. Know where your companions are. Know your gun and ammo. Be sure of your target and what's beyond. Alcohol and shooting don't mix! Put on the safety switch.

—March 2, 1991, Mead Composition notebook of
Karanding *Baratunde Thurston*

IN THE absence of my father, my mother was always searching for men to add to my life. The whole effort had a "Who's Your Father Figure?" game show feel to it. One week, I'd be hanging out with James West, an old family friend, musician, and photographer. He taught me how to use a camera and encouraged my musical interests. He worked as a bicycle courier, owned massive fish tanks, and lived one block away. He was on the top (fourth) floor of his building and had no buzzer. This was pre–mobile phones, so when we went to visit, we simply stood on the sidewalk on 16th Street, aimed our heads high, and yelled, in concert, at the top of our lungs, "Yo James!! Jaaaaaames West!!!!" Every. Time. Some children are discouraged from hollering in the street. For me, it was a regularly scheduled family activity.

In another week, I might spend time with Pepe and Pinky, the Latino owners of a local bike shop called Brothers & Bicycles. They gave me extra bass lessons and sold my mother my first bike. When we went to pick it up, my mother made me sign a hand-written contract witnessed by both Pepe and Pinky, stating that I would never let anyone else ride my bike, and if I did, I would have to forfeit it to her. I wondered what she would do with a bike made for a ten-year-old boy, but I never tested the terms of our agreement to find out.

The individual men my mother brought into my life rode, sold, and fixed bicycles. They played all manner of instruments. They were photographers and booksellers, and one was even a Buddhist. All of them served to subconsciously round out my definition of what black and brown men could be and do, and I owe part of my present-day love of cycling, music, photography, and books to these men. But my mother's most significant attempt to fill the man void in my upbringing was my enrollment in the Ankobia program at the same time as she enrolled me at Sidwell Friends.

"Ankobia" is a term from the Twi language of Ghana, which

means "vanguard" or "those who lead in battle." It is also the name of an Afrocentric "rites of passage" program I completed during my early teen years in DC. I like to think of it as a counterweight to the elite private education I received five days a week on the other side of town. It was Hebrew school for blackness.

Established by Pan-African black American activists, Ankobia was designed to help black children make the transition into adulthood and withstand the assaults and temptations of life in the crack-ridden city in the 1990s. Think of it like an extended bar mitzvah minus the dance party, expensive gifts, and belief in the one true God. Then add an element of Scared Straight. Every Saturday from seven a.m. until just after noon, I would gather with a dozen or so other black boys (we were called *karanding*, which is Kiswahili for "student") at the Nationhouse Watoto School in Northwest Washington. There we would engage in rigorous physical exercise, practical life-skills training, and black history education.

The physical training was intense. It was led by a massive and fit man we called Baba Mike.* He led us in a routine that included a thousand jumping jacks, scores of push-ups, martial arts techniques, and an agonizing abdominal exercise involving us lying on our backs and lifting our feet six inches off the ground for several seconds at a time. In the bonus round of this latter exercise, Baba Mike would yell, "Six inches up!" and then *walk* on our abdomens.

The life-skills education covered the practical. We got les-

---

* *Baba* basically means "father," and it is how we addressed all the adult men.

sons in carpentry and electrical work, and we were taught how to operate firearms safely. When I look back, there's something potentially horrifying about this latter lesson, but at the time, it felt as natural as the former. The odds were high that we would be exposed to guns at some point, and we might as well know how to handle them.

The primary education we received, however, was mental and cultural. We had a reading list that included the work or biographies of Malcolm X, Martin Luther King Jr., Paul Robeson, Kwame Nkrumah, Toussaint L'Ouverture, Frederick Douglass, and Nat Turner. We were exposed to West African elders, who explained their religious and cultural traditions. We learned to dance to the drum. We ate couscous! And we were pushed to question the values of the mainstream society around us.

I remember one Saturday sitting in the classroom, possibly discussing *The Isis Papers* by Dr. Frances Cress Welsing, when one of the *baba*s called out a boy from Baltimore. The kid was wearing a Los Angeles Raiders NFL Starter jacket. These were the height of cool at the time. The *baba*, referring to the team logo on the front of the jacket, pointedly asked him, "Brother, why are you wearing *that white man* over your heart?" None of us thought of Starter jackets that way. We then all got a lecture on economic self-determination, trans-Atlantic slave trading, and the importance of symbolism.

As I mentioned, I was in this program at the same time as I was enrolled at Sidwell Friends. I think my mother loved the idea of combining two extreme educational influences that would, in fact, check each other. Too much exposure to Sidwell's culture, and I might forget where I came from, start to value things foreign to my upbringing, and end up a total disappointment to my community by joining the Republican Party—this was unlikely, given Sidwell's Quaker origins, but still. Too much exposure to the Ankobia world, though, might have me thinking black folk were only kings and queens, and white folk could never ever be trusted. This is clearly not true, as I trust some of my best white friends to help me get cabs on a regular basis.

The whole Ankobia experience felt like a Black Power boot camp with young brown men trained in self-defense and the handling of firearms, given books that told a more complete version of their history, and shown that they are beautiful children of the universe. The combination of these Saturday sessions with my Sidwell experiences would lead to tense and hilarious results on occasion.

░░░░░░░░░░░░░░░░░░░░░░░░░░

The U.S. Propaganda Machine: A Middle School Paper

THE BLACKNESS-BOLSTERING Ankobia rites-of-passage experience had strong effects on my perspective and behavior at Sidwell. As initiates, my fellow *karanding* and I were expected to behave almost like fraternity brothers away from the Saturday sessions. Every day we were required to wear a leather medallion featuring a red, black, and green pattern. This medallion served to physically remind me of the Saturday lessons even while I peeled bar mitzvah invitations from the inside of my school locker across town. Given the popularity of Afrocentric hip-hop at the time—groups like Brand Nubian and Poor Righteous Teachers were exploding then—no one at Sidwell thought much of my adornment. But on occasion, the Ankobia perspective would find its way into my school activities.

In high school, as head of the Black Student Union, I helped write a report to the board of trustees on the status of life for students of color. We documented cases of discriminatory applications of discipline, and called for more black faculty and a more diverse curriculum. We titled it "The Students of Color Report." We were very original. But well before I channeled my blackness into approved campus political activity and congressional commission– style documents, the Ankobia experience dramatically influenced my academic work. Such was the case in March of 1991.

I was in the eighth grade and had a paper due for my English class. I cannot recall the specific assignment, but I'm sure the paper I submitted missed the teacher's expectations by a wide margin. Using Microsoft Word on Windows version 3.0, I wrote the paper as if it were a major speech I planned to deliver to all black people in the United States. I printed it out on my dot-matrix printer, and on March 9, 1991, handed over the following 1,100-word address:*

The Destruction of Afrikans : The U.S. Propaganda Machine

I am here today, my Afrikan brothers and sisters, to speak on a very serious problem of our people. We are in a state of emergency, and headed downward fast.

I am here today, my Afrikan brothers and sisters, first, to make you aware of the problem, and second, to help you deal with and try to solve it.

As many of you know, we have been hit by a serious epidemic, this epidemic is (at least in this country) is the destruction of our people, by our people. One can rarely miss a day without hearing

---

* I have kept all spelling, grammar, and punctuation true to the original 1991 formatting, especially the spelling of "Afrikan" with a K, because it's awesome.

about some black man killing another black man, or some black husband murdering his wife for trying to divorce him. And while we hear daily reports of blacks being killed, the whites, sometimes subconsciously are shaking hands and patting each other on the back for a job well done. Some people may say: "Well. why don't you just tell them to stop!" Now, I thank those people for their input; but I have one thing to say about that suggestion: it's not that easy! As Marcus Garvey once said: "The best offense you can use against the Negro is disorganization."

Well, Mr. Garvey had a point there.

Now, my brothers and sisters, I will tell you ways that. the white man has led our people into this epidemic. If you want to go way back:

It all started when the Europeans invaded our rich, prosperous motherland, and robbed her of her people. At the time of the slave trade, there were Africans who sold their own people for beads and jewelry. This was the beginning of our self destruction.

Another possibility is found by looking at the brutal times of slavery. During slavery some of the brutalities were earthshaking and unfathomable. We were treated as livestock, whipped like horses, chained like animals, and auctioned like estate, not to mention the treatment, and raping of our women. Families were separated, and we were made to abandon our native languages, and made to erase our beautiful culture, and made ignorant. During all these years, the tension was building up to one day reach a climax or peak. Well, my brothers and sisters, we have reached dooms day. Now you would hope that we would take out our hostilities on the whites, after all they did put us in this situation. But no, we were made so ignorant that we're taking it out on ourselves, OURSELVES!?

*And yet, my brothers and sisters, another time the white man
had forced us into this epidemic was the time after slavery, when
he displayed his demonic evil self even more. After slavery we were
fooled more, and made even more ignorant. I come to this conclusion
because they told us we were free ("they" being the white man).
They fooled us into believing that we were free and equal to them.
Most of us did not know much about freedom, except that which
we limitedly heard about the "north." Being in such the state that
we were, anyone could say we were free and we would believe it.
because we didn't even know what freedom was. This was and is
one of many ways that the white man has taken advantage of our
naiveté.*

*The fourth and final way that the white man has forced us into
this deadly virus of self-destruction is by way of what is known as the
"U.S. Propaganda Machine."*

*First, let's begin with a definition of propaganda; as defined by
Marcus Garvey:*

*" . . . organized methods used to control the world is the thing
known and called 'PROPAGANDA.'*

*Propaganda has done more to defeat the good intentions of races
and nations than even open warfare.*

*Propaganda is a method or medium used by organized peoples
to convert others against their will.*

*We of the Negro race are suffering more than any other race in
the world from propaganda—Propaganda to destroy our hopes, our
ambitions our confidence . . ." and eventually ourselves.*

*America has come up with different techniques to keep us down,
from segregation to prejudice, there's always been something new. In
a way things were better during and immediately following slavery,*

because at least then whites told you what they thought. But now racism is more virulent. Now whites say we are equal, and pat us on the shoulder, and eat with us, and act all goody goody. They even allow us in their government to show us how equal we are. But under that Kentucky cotton coating there is still the feeling, solid as the Rockies that we are inferior. Back then there was absolutely no way we could argue against a white man's word, we weren't even allowed to "fight." Nowadays we're allowed to speak in their courts and they occasionally let us win, just to show us that we're equal. That's like letting us fight but they have the weapon, and one out of a hundred times we can knock the weapon out of their hand and get a good punch in to knock them out; The problem was just stated, we're just knocking them out, when we need to kill them.

The "U.S. Propaganda Machine" has three major outlets into the Afrikan community. They are the church, the school, and the mass media.

The church is part of the "Propaganda Machine" through its teaching of a white Jesus. Some, if even a few people know of Africa's greatness as having the first trace of civilization. But if people knew that and the fact that the Bible says Adam was the first, logic would tell you that Adam was African.

The schools are involved in the Propaganda Machine through their teaching, or should I say their nonteaching of African and African-American history. Considering Afrikan's great contribution to this country's wealth, not only in slave labor but in inventions such as the signal light and in medicine. The least this country could do is give us an "honorable mention."

Third, mass media is involved by means of its portrayal of whites as superior. Since the beginning of television whites held

*the foreground. They were shown on horseback shooting down
"uncivilized" Indians and taming the "cannibalistic and wild" ways
of Africans. And when we finally were on the television, it was as
a negative depiction. They did not show us as the "first," they did
not show us as the geniuses we were, nor did they show our great
heritage. The only thing they could find were our "backwards and
primitive" ways. The mass media has played an extensive role in the
destruction of our people.*

*Lastly, my Afrikan brothers and sisters I have something to tell
you. Beware of the white man; I'm not saying to be scared of him or
to cut off communication, but beware, because when we realize that
we should not be fighting each other, the tide will turn.*

I was thirteen years old when I wrote that and handed it in
to my English teacher. If a middle school student turned in such
a document today, he would immediately be sent to a counselor
or detention facility, but this was pre-Columbine 1991. The number one song on the *Billboard* charts was the upbeat *Someday* by
Mariah Carey, and the top television show was *Cheers*. It was a
happier time.

After class the next day, my teacher pulled me aside to discuss my manifesto. "You would never have written this if I weren't
black, would you?" he asked. I responded, "Absolutely *not*, and I
trust you to keep my secret!"

The White Student Union

SOMETIMES WHITE people just like to ask questions. They don't mean anything by it. There are no judgments in it. They just want to know, and what's wrong with asking questions?

My mother returned from the Sidwell Friends parents association meeting livid. They had been discussing the prom and how it would be financed, and one of the parents (a white parent) had offhandedly asked, "Well, doesn't the Black Student Union have a lot of money?"

See, she was just asking a question!

Indeed the Black Student Union did have "a lot of money," which we raised through one massive, heavily coordinated, expensively secured annual dance party known as The BSU Go-Go.*

---

* Go-Go is a type of music unique to Washington, DC. It involves drums. Many black people love it. White people love it, too. People not from DC hate it. For more information on the genre, search YouTube.

Exactly what those funds had to do with the prom was unclear to my mother, and the inference that the BSU would somehow cover the costs of this school-wide event offended her. However, that parent didn't directly demand the money. She was just asking a question.

Sidwell was a school populated in part by the children of Washington's liberal elite. There were lawyers and senators and lobbyists and White House administration officials among the parent class. Being loyal NPR listeners and Clinton voters, many of these parents thought they were incapable of even a hint of racism. They voted for Bill Clinton! He was the first "black president." Their children had black friends! So they felt insulated from even the possibility that they might display racist tendencies.

Fortunately, the treasury of the Black Student Union was not pilfered by the creative financing concepts of this particular parent, but "questions" challenging the legitimacy of black communities were a regular occurrence.

One such question revolved around the informal institution of black kids eating together in the cafeteria. I'm going to let you in on a secret: growing black children like to eat. In a majority-white school, they are often friends with other black people. This has been known to result in black kids eating together at the same table. While this terrorist cell–like activity is a perceived clear and present danger to some in the non-black community, the agenda at most of these nefarious, exclusive gatherings consisted of talking about classes, flirting, making fun of each other, and, oh, plotting the downfall of White America—but only on every third Tuesday.

Preparing to inherit the rights and privileges of their race later in life, many white students were put off by the unspoken exclusivity of "the black table." Due to our limited camouflage abilities—most of us still wore the dark skin into which we were born—"the black table" visually stood out in ways gatherings of other groups (the A/V kids, football players, or Future Corporate Douchebags of America) might not have. In addition, the Civil Rights Movement was over, so what's with the sit-in-looking gathering? This confusion and offense led to a question: Why do all the black kids sit at the same lunch table?

The best answer exists itself in the form of a question: Why do all the *white* students sit together at the same tables? No one ever asked that, because such seating arrangements were "normal." You don't question ten tables of nearly all white children dining. You question the one or two with nearly all black children dining.

Questions implying that a black student group should not be able to control its money or that forced desegregation at cafeteria tables might be needed were notable among the set of White People Questions I experienced at Sidwell. However, my favorite by far was the following:

Why don't we have a White Student Union?

I remember the student who asked this. She was confused by the existence of "students of color" meetings and the Black Student Union. The idea that there were official organizations, sanctioned by the school, based around racial identity, was offensive and wrong, and so she just "asked a question," which was: "Why don't we have a White Student Union?"

My mind immediately flashed to previous iterations of "white student unions": white citizens' councils, Ku Klux Klan rallies, and Dave Matthews Band concerts, but she didn't mean anything so sinister. She simply didn't get why white students were not allowed to self-identify by race and gather regularly, in a semi-exclusive fashion, for the advancement of their interests.

No one told her that the entire school was essentially a White Student Union.

How to Be The Black Friend

So FAR, I've painted a picture of myself as this tiny, hard-core, militant black kid, and in truth I was that way, but I wasn't *only* that way. As with all children, I was trying on points of view and personalities, imitating what I saw around me, and figuring out just what "being myself" actually meant. I carried the banner of black justice as loudly as I waved the flags of pop culture, adolescent crushes, genuine friendliness, and a desire to be liked by the people around me. The first two years at Sidwell, seventh and eighth grades, were the toughest period of cultural adjustment, but as with all exposure to new languages, immersion worked, and over time, I felt as at home on the sidelines of a field hockey match as I did in a West African drum circle.

After seventh grade, my mother decided to move us off of Newton Street in DC. She had fought the good fight against the steady takeover of our neighborhood by drug dealers and users, and she was losing. We all were. I recall her returning one evening from a peace vigil organized by St. Stephen's Episcopal church across the street. Some of the young hustlers thought it would be fun to egg the candle-wielding activists and demonstrate who was really in charge, so when my mother returned, she was covered in egg.

Another morning, I looked through our front window only to notice that a bullet had pierced two panes of the triple-paned glass. The shot came from a BB gun, but the fact that it wasn't a real gun didn't make my mother feel any better. Through all of this, I was generally as happy as could be. The occasional police raid, mass brawl, and steady drug traffic didn't bother me too much. It felt normal, and that is probably what frightened my mother the most. So she moved us out to Takoma Park, Maryland, to a single-family home with a massive deck and even more massive front yard. With long, extracurricular-heavy school days, a one-hour public transit commute on both ends, and limited time in my new friendless neighborhood, my social life was increasingly defined by Sidwell, which meant I had white friends! I had black friends, too, but the numbers made *not* having white friends nearly impossible, and these friendships offered new opportunities to share my blackness with others, not always voluntarily.

It began with my hair. White schoolmates would look at my afro, then shout excitedly, "Is that your real hair?" and "That is so cool!" and "Can I touch it?" all the while *reaching* to touch it regardless of what answer was percolating from my mind to my mouth in response to their perfunctory inquiry. If I did not know you, the answer was simply, "No!" accompanied by a gracefully evasive maneuver to avoid unsanctioned hand-to-hair contact. But if we were friends, I would offer a detailed response. I would patiently explain that it was rude to just touch someone's hair without permission; that black people, especially, have a history of white people exerting their privilege over black bodies, extending from uninvited head-rubbing to far worse transgressions; that it was disgusting, considering how many people don't wash their hands after using the restroom. Now armed with inside information, these white friends of mine were more respectful of my perspective and sometimes explained the logic to their own white friends on their own initiative!*

Hair was just the beginning. First at Sidwell, then later at Harvard and in various workplaces, I learned just how important and powerful the role of black-friend-to-white-people could be. Now, I'm going to share some of those valuable lessons with you.

You are about to learn how to be The Black Friend.

Move through this chapter with the weight of America's history and future upon your shoulders, and treat the lesson with the same respect you might reserve for an original copy of the Constitution or perhaps Bob Hope's DNA. The Black Friend is that important to the United States.

The Black Friend has value to all non-black Americans but especially white Americans. By having a Black Friend, white Americans automatically inoculate themselves against most charges of racism and capture some of the rebellious spirit that has made this country what it is. They become cooler by association.

Here's how all these benefits might play out in one setting. First, a white person brings her Black Friend to a party, adding

---

* Some of my non-American friends have assured me that hair-touching is quite common across ethnic lines in their own countries, to which I respond, "This. Is. America!" and then kick them into a giant pit as if we lived in ancient Sparta.

instant cultural credibility to the event. There may be a little extra buzz in the room. Second, that white person has more latitude to speak ignorance of a racial nature by invoking the fact that she "has a black friend." Innocence-by-association is a powerful defensive tactic. Depending on the type of household she is from, it may be forbidden or at least frowned upon to go hanging around with black folks. So the white person who brings her Black Friend home can enjoy the added benefit of rebelling against her parents. The Black Friend is a cultural Swiss Army knife for many white Americans, able to perform several functions of both a stylistic and practical nature.

While The Black Friend's value to White America is long established and readily apparent upon slight reflection, it's The Black Friend's value to *Black* America that is truly underappreciated. Yes, The Black Friend is the best friend of Black America.

First, The Black Friend is a key intelligence asset, like a CIA operative, both transmitting and receiving valuable information that continually helps prevent a race war by increasing understanding, lowering tensions, and offering diplomatic back channels.

A well-trained Black Friend can learn the ways of White America without hyperbole or judgment but instead based on actual lived experiences. For example, a good Black Friend can see the artistic merit in Nirvana's "Smells Like Teen Spirit" rather than dismiss it as simply "a bunch of white people music." A truly insightful Black Friend may even see the song as essentially hip-hop in nature, if one were to really think about it with an open mind.*

---

* Seriously, this song is amazing. Give it a chance!

This same Black Friend can also explain the line between curiosity and an accidental hate crime, say, by telling her white friends that it is not okay to just go up to a black person and touch her hair.

By acting as a buffer and a sounding board between worlds, The Black Friend can prevent misunderstandings from escalating into an all-out conflagration, and all black people benefit from these quiet acts of diplomacy, not just those who serve as Black Friends. The irony is that many in the black community look with derision upon those of their number who serve as Black Friends. Truly exceptional Black Friends are treated as traitors to their race, told they aren't "black enough," and called Oreos and sellouts. If you are the type of person to instantly judge a black person seemingly enjoying himself in the company of a group of white people, think twice before you judge. He just might be on a mission!

If only Black America knew the sacrifices Black Friends make every single day to preserve the peace, we would erect monuments and memorials in their honor. We would call for a moment of silence during the BET Awards, or better yet, replace the awards with a three-hour moment of silence for our too-silent defenders and advocates.

During the Cold War, U.S. and Russian leaders installed a special direct communications device that came to be known as the "red telephone." They would use it to talk to each other in secret, explaining military movements and other actions that could be misinterpreted as acts of war. Black Friends are our red telephones. They are our covert agents. They are interracial code breakers, and in the Cold War, we had a name for the men and women on both sides of the conflict performing these functions. They saved lives every day with no expectation of recognition except by the few who knew their true names. We called them heroes. That's what Black Friends are: heroes. America's heroes.

YOUR BLACK FRIEND TOOL SET

Now that you grasp the importance of this role, here are some key traits and assets you must possess to serve as a good Black Friend.

Cultural authenticity

You won't be of much value to black people or anyone else if you don't maintain a cultural connection to black experiences. Like a reporter who clings to the newsroom rather than step outside and actually walk his beat, you will lose your effectiveness. In a practical sense, this means you need to maintain a baseline level of black cultural currency by being familiar with at least some of the history of black people, of trends in black entertainment—this goes for music, film, sports, et cetera—as well as language and style. You don't need to overdo it by trying to be "too black," but if you're not seen as black enough, no one will buy your story, and you won't get the inside access that makes your role so valuable.

Physical authenticity

This is not about how you look. It's about how you act. Intellectual knowledge of black culture will only get you so far in your service. You must also be able to do black things. Ideally, you will be fairly competent in at least one of the following areas: rapping, dancing, grilling or frying meats, and running or other stereotypically black sports. If you can back up your mental knowledge of blackness with an occasional Moon (or Crip) Walk and a semiannual freestyle rhyme, your value is assured. Again, this is about appearances to maintain your cover.

A sense of humor

A good Black Friend doesn't take any remark or experience too seriously, but remember that balance is key. There is a risk associated with not taking things seriously enough. Your effectiveness depends on your ability to make non-black people feel comfortable. You can't go flying off the handle every time something potentially racist goes down. If you do that, you risk losing the privileged position of Black Friend and sliding into the much less useful role of Angry Negro (see "How to Be The Angry Negro"). Angry Negroes have a role in our society, but they have much less freedom of mobility, and this chapter is about the diplomatic art of Black Friendship, so let's stay true to that mission.

Just because you're an uncelebrated secret agent and diplomat doesn't mean you can't have fun. One entertaining way to keep your friends on their toes is to occasionally play the race card for fun. For example, if you're getting in the car with them and you end up being directed to the backseat, you can yell, "Why do I have to sit in the back? Is it because I'm black!?" They'll be nervous for a moment, but then you'll laugh, and they'll laugh, and oh, the fun times you can have being The Black Friend.

Patience

You're going to get a lot of questions. Many of them will be dumb. Most will be some variation on "Is this racist?" Maintain your cool, and focus on listening to your friends. When they ask, "Why don't more black people work hard like immigrants?"

don't assume bad intentions on their part. Stop. Breathe. Think. What are they really saying with this question? They are doing a surface-level comparison. They see Group A and Group B. To them, both groups have experienced similar setbacks, but Group B doesn't seem to have made nearly as much progress as Group A in the recovery. This is not automatically racist. They're asking you because they trust you, because they *need* you to help them understand. If you scare them away, you encourage a troubling alternative. Instead of taking that seemingly dumb question to you, their trusted Black Friend, they will continue to live with their ignorance, which will eventually find its way into the news segments they produce at their television network jobs or into legislation they pass. A healthy amount of patience as The Black Friend can go a long way toward helping all black people in unseen ways.

Access to white people

You can't very well be a good Black Friend if you don't have access to non-black, and especially white, people. This should go without saying, but I can't tell you the number of black folks I've met who want nothing to do with white people and yet complain nonstop about how white people do this or white people think that. Be the change you want to see. Go make some white friends. If you don't know where to start, I recommend checking out *Stuff White People Like*, the website or book. It's all right there for the understanding.

This list is not exhaustive, but it's a representative sample of the set of tools you will need to perform your duties. If you carry these with you, you will make an excellent Black Friend and do your people, black, white, and otherwise, proud. There is just one more thing:*

BEWARE OTHER BLACK PEOPLE

As I've documented in the history of The Black Friend, many black people do not respect this role and many more don't even know we have blacks deployed in this fashion at all. That can make for some awkward interactions when you're with your white friends and come across this type of black person. Keep in mind, they mean no harm. They just don't understand the mission you're on, so remain calm, careful, and vigilant. There are ways to minimize the damage done by these potentially hostile inter-Negro interactions.

Always acknowledge other black people. If you are overly focused on your Black Friend duties, you might miss the presence of another black person. *They* will see *you*. They always see you. You stand out in your crowd, and they will test you, usually by catching your eye, then offering an upward or downward head nod. Depending on your gender, the test might stop at eye contact or progress to a polite smile. It's like in the movie *Avatar*† when they say, "I see you."

Your worst mistake here would be to see the other black person, let them see you seeing them, then fail to acknowledge them. You come across as too good for your own people, and you end

---

* Welcome to my Columbo moment. There's always "one more thing" with that guy.

† By the way, *Avatar* is a truly horrible movie. The worst white guy ever somehow manages to be the best blue person ever, just like that? Come on now. If I lived in that world, I'd have to write *How to Be Blue*, because the tale is basically the same.

up making things harder for yourself by creating or furthering a feeling of distrust, and without trust, we have nothing.

You also want to keep an active eye on the behavior of your white friends when other non–Black Friends are around. If you're doing your job, your white friends will be extremely comfortable and loose in your presence. This is generally a good thing, but it can lead to embarrassment if your white friends are dropping a lot of black slang, rap lyrics, or worst of all, the words "nigga" or "nigger."

As a general rule, *never* allow your white friends to say any variation of the word "nigger" but especially in the company of others. It is your job to explain to them why such statements are unacceptable. You can appeal to history. You can explain the continuing pain associated with the term. You can cite family-style in-group versus out-group privileges. Do what you must. The good news is that they will listen to you in a way they would never listen to a random black person they don't know.

When you hear white people ask, "Why is it okay for black people to say the N-word and not me?" those white people are missing a good Black Friend in their lives.

How to Speak for All Black People

MY OWN experiences as The Black Friend were merely training exercises for a much larger role. In the classroom, workplace, and beyond, once you're known as someone who is willing to talk about race, you become an official spokesperson for your race. Often your *willingness* isn't actually required. Your mere standing as a member of the group in question is taken as qualification enough. Many a black person has been blindsided by the "what do you think about [insert potentially black-related topic here]?" question. Not thinking about the consequences, the non-black person asking simply reaches for the closest representative he or she can find, but for those unprepared for the call of duty, it can be a traumatic experience, leading to episodes of self-doubt, anger, and dry skin. Where this demand for black spokespeople is acute, however, is in the media.

As a blogger, public speaker, and black-person-who-writes-books-with-the-word-"black"-in-the-title, I've had my fair share of media exposure playing some version of the black spokesperson game. There's usually some kind of blackness emergency in which the cable networks light up a black version of the Bat-signal, hailing any and all potentially credible voices to offer perspective. Sometimes that beam is directed toward me, but unlike Batman, I don't feel the need to respond to every hail. I remember one particularly urgent-sounding invitation from a network.

"[Former Illinois governor Rod] Blagojevich just said he's blacker than Obama! Can you come in?"

"Well, when?"

"Now!"

"No, thanks for thinking of me, but I can't make it in for this one. Maybe next time."

I bet half the calls Batman responds to are situations people could work out for themselves by employing basic common sense. If I had accepted that invitation to comment on the Blagojevich segment, I would have gone on air, said, "This is dumb," then sat in silence for the rest of the segment checking my Twitter messages. This would have wasted the network's time, but more important, *my* time. Still, even though I'm occasionally part of the system, that system leaves a lot to be desired.

Faced with declining profit margins, fierce competition from a multiplication of news outlets, and continuing consolidation, the media is barely able to gather and analyze facts (see: pre–Iraq War coverage, housing bubble, the financial crisis, the *continuing* financial crisis, et cetera), much less discuss issues of race in an intelligent manner. Add to their general ineptitude an abysmally low level of diversity among editors and producers at the major media outlets, and you can see why they are so often forced to import "black" experts. Whether about the president's supposedly anti-American pastor, a black athlete's criminality, or the probably racist statements of a white public figure, the U.S. media is continuously searching for a black voice to explain black people. In their ideal world, exactly one Representative of Blackness would hold a national black press conference every few weeks to answer all black-related questions:

- Why do black people riot?
- Is it true you all hate homosexuals?
- What do you have against hockey?
- Et cetera, et cetera.

But with so many competitive news outlets and so many questions, this is not logistically possible. Every network wants its own black spokesperson, and the Reverends Jesse and Al can only cover so much ground.

In this chapter, I will teach you how to take advantage of the booming black spokesperson market and provide a valuable service to the nation's clueless media outlets. Here is a list of what you'll need to be successful:

PART 1—APPEARANCE

Be male

Overlooking the contributions and perspectives of black women is essential to the media narrative of the black experience. For women who are serious about pursuing this line of work, focus on identifying an appropriate black male to represent you to the media.

Have slogans

Make sure they rhyme. What do Jesse Jackson and R. Kelly have in common? They are both powerful black spokesmen, and they rhyme. Never underestimate the media's hunger for a rhyming Negro.

Speak clearly

However, don't enunciate too well. Try not to say "however," for example. Perfect diction may undermine your black cred. The media will only accept a handful of black spokespeople who sound like they went to the same schools as them.

Don't be too young or too old

The ideal black spokesperson is thirty-five to sixty years old. Toward the younger end, they are looking for the voice of the next generation. On the older end, it's about getting the perspective of civil rights veterans. Once you get too far above sixty, however, you don't play as well for the camera, and you start sounding crazy (see: Bill Cosby).

Wear a suit

Always wear a suit. The media absolutely loves a black man in a suit. It says you mean business. A confusing racial situation can break out at any moment, and you never know when you might get the call, so wear one constantly whether sleeping, jogging, or mowing your lawn. In an emergency, say the complete flooding and near-destruction of a major American city, a tracksuit can be substituted, but only in an emergency.

PART 2—THE BLACK RÉSUMÉ

For television appearances, the producer or host must be able to cite you as someone deeply in touch with the black experience. Below, we offer a multiple-choice, credibility-establishing résumé template to get you started.

Please select one option from each of the following experience areas:

FOUNDED:

1. The National Coalition for Operation
2. Operation: National Coalition
3. The Coalition for National Operation

LED PROTESTS FOLLOWING:

1. The brutal police shooting of an unarmed black man
2. Any black person's allegations of racial violence by whites
3. The release of yet another Tyler Perry movie

IS A LONGTIME CIVIL RIGHTS ACTIVIST WHO:

1. Marched with Dr. Martin Luther King Jr.
2. Saw Dr. Martin Luther King Jr. marching on television
3. Bought chips at a corner store on Martin Luther King Jr. Boulevard in a major U.S. city

So, if your name is "Joe Smith," your television intro would go something like this.

To help us understand the situation, we'd like to go to Joe Smith. Joe, of course, is the founder of Operation: National Coalition, once saw Dr. Martin Luther King

*Jr. marching on television, and led protests following the
release of the movie* Madea's Family Reunion. *Thanks for
joining us, Joe* . . .

PART 3—BLACK ISSUES

There are two types of issues: those that have to do with black
people and everything else. You must be prepared to comment
on both. The following is a media-approved list of official black
issues:

- Crime. Why do black people do so much?
- Affirmative action. Why do black people take jobs from
  white people?
- Poverty. Why are black people poor?
- Racism. Why haven't black people gotten over it already?
- Drugs. Why do black people do them?
- Sunflower seeds. Why do black people love them?
- Welfare. Why are black people on it?
- Hip-hop. Why can't black people just let us have it
  already? Come on! Gimme!
- The Black Vote. Who are *all* the black people voting for?
- Obama. Do you still like him?

Because all black people also double as black issues, be prepared to discuss any prominent black figure, including:

- Oprah. What is she doing right now?
- Kanye West. Why is he so rude?
- Michelle Obama. She can dance!

- Bill Cosby. Why is he so angry?
- Louis Farrakhan. He's still your official leader, right? Defend his latest extreme statement.
- LeBron James. Why, God, why???
- Any other black person, dead or alive.

You might wonder if it's your role to talk about issues that have no connection to race or blackness, but if you're going to be an effective spokesperson for Black America, it's up to you to create that connection. If you find yourself in the media spotlight, being asked about nuclear proliferation or Riverdance, don't panic. You got this. Just remember your training. Invoke your résumé, adjust your suit, and bring it back to blackness. Your career depends on it.

PART 4—GETTING MEDIA TO NOTICE YOU

As with money, it takes media coverage to get media coverage. To get on TV you need to have been on TV. Confused? Pay attention. You have three key tasks.

1. Be ready for the media

In today's 24/7, always-connected society, a celebrity could say something about your people or urban police could torture a black man at any moment. In fact, while you're studying this guide, something very black is going down, and you're missing it. You are off to a terrible start.

2. Monitor your world for any opportunity to speak blackly

Reading newspapers is optional. Watching television is critical, especially cable news. Listening to talk radio is nice, but reading blogs is better. The beauty of the Internet is that you don't have to wait for a racially tense incident to happen. You just have to search for one. YouTube is essentially a racism-on-demand video service available, free of charge, at any hour of the day. When you find an opportunity, ask yourself, which black issue is at stake? If none, which one can be injected? Also, *are you wearing your suit?*

3. Build your own media presence

The first opportunity you find to test your spokesperson skills may not generate the major media coverage it deserves. You need to start by generating your own. Here are some ideas:

- Start a newsletter. The name of it is not important, but the motto should be "Voice of the People."

- Get a radio show. The fact that you have a show is all that matters. What you say and whether or not it's true is unimportant, so long as you keep talking!

- Blog! All the time! You should post at least twelve times a day. It does not matter what you blog about. Trust me.

- Have several people follow you around with a camera. Occasionally stop in front of government buildings and issue statements. Again, what you say is not important, only that you capture it on camera.

PART 5—HATING ON OTHER BLACK PEOPLE

A big part of your job as Spokesperson for Black America may be to hate on other black people, especially those who pose a threat to your standing. I recommend the following tactics:

- Challenge their blackness and claim they are out of touch, especially by asserting that a white person is blacker than they are.

- Accuse them of being racist and acting against the interests of black people.

- Spread one of their controversial, out-of-context sound bites that makes it sound like they said something exactly the opposite of what you know they said.*

BONUS—THE ALTERNATIVE CONSERVATIVE PATH

Let's face it. By following my advice, you will become a spokesperson for Black America, but you'll make it by playing the traditional role of aggrieved liberal Negro expected by the media. What I've shown above works, but it's also uninspired and unoriginal. If you are serious about making a mark, and *money*, then consider playing the part of Conservative Black Spokesperson.

The key to success as a Conservative Black Spokesperson is to

---

* For example, you could grab a clip of the person saying she intentionally discriminated against a white farmer from her government position even though the full video makes it clear this statement was a setup to a larger point about how such discrimination was wrong.

take the "Hating on Other Black People" section on the previous page and build your entire strategy on that one element.

Your explanation for every media-approved black issue is quite simple. You just blame black pathology. For example, while it may be true that substance abuse occurs at a lower rate among young blacks than whites but rises to outweigh whites later in life,* there is no market for that kind of fact-based commentary, and you will quickly find yourself out of a job if you insist on repeating such nonsense. Your job is to blame Black America for the drug problem, crime, homelessness, unemployment, the price of oil, and the budget deficit. Most important, you must attribute such negative behaviors to an innate dysfunction within the black psyche.

If you're asked to comment on a black public figure, don't hesitate to extrapolate his or her negative behavior to the entire black population. If a black professional athlete severely injures a clubgoer, it's just another example of the hyperviolent nature of black men. You should use this case as a launching point to criticize single-parent households and more black pathology.

You *cannot* overexploit these opportunities. It's simply not possible.

If you find yourself running out of ways to blame black people, use any of the following tactics to distract your host:

- Invoke the success of minority immigrants who came here voluntarily.

---

* "Blacks have lower rates of substance use and abuse than whites in early adolescence and young adulthood but similar or higher rates by middle adulthood . . ."
—January–February 2011 issue of *Sociological Spectrum*, in article titled "Black-White Differences in Aging Out of Substance Use and Abuse"

- Cite the number of decades since the end of slavery.
- Blame hip-hop.
- Point to the example of Barack Obama.
- Blame hip-hop again.

This technique works whether for anti–affirmative action crusaders of the 1990s or black Tea Party members of the 2010s. Whichever black spokesperson path you choose, conservative or traditional, take pride in the fact that both can be equally unhelpful to your people.

BEYOND THE MEDIA

In all likelihood, you won't be called to perform such a high-profile task as representing all black people in the media, but you can still use this training in your everyday life. Scale the lessons down. Most of them still apply to smaller contexts, like drinks with coworkers or hanging out with non-black friends. Inevitably, someone in this group will ask you, "Dayshawn"—your name is Dayshawn to these people—"what do you think about [black issue x]?" Know that by "you" they mean "all black people everywhere," and answer appropriately.

Your answer may not be broadcast live on cable news, but it is no less important. You never know who among your non-black friends and colleagues will end up writing black characters for a TV show or movie, so answer carefully! The fate of the race depends on you.

(See the chapters "How to Be The Black Friend" and "How to Be The Black Employee" to further sharpen your skills as racial representative.)

Have You Ever Wanted to *Not* Be Black?

SPEAKING ON behalf of black people, being The Black Friend, understanding your place on the scales of blackness—all this can be quite exhausting. Sometimes, and for any number of reasons, you don't want to be black anymore, even if just for a moment.

There can be a certain mental overhead that accompanies being black, and it isn't always welcome. When I asked The Black Panel about this phenomenon, most admitted to, at one point or another, wanting to distance themselves from or even renounce their membership in Team Black America.

DAMALI AYO

I had a little bit of a "want to be Korean" phase in college. I straightened my hair, I was dying it black,* hanging out with Koreans. That lasted for a couple of months.

---

* Her natural hair color is brown.

CHERYL CONTEE

In terms of "Are there times when I have wished that I wasn't black?" no, there aren't times. Certainly I've experienced real discrimination in my life, discrimination that has impacted my career and my social life, and that has been painful.

There's a young man who basically told me he wasn't going to marry me because his family said, "Just don't marry a nigger." That was really painful to live through, like a hundred times more painful, dehumanizing, humiliating than it sounds, but I didn't wish that I wasn't black when that happened, or when I found out that I was getting paid less, like $20,000 less, than a white guy who was reporting to me.

It didn't make me wish that I wasn't black. It just made me really angry and frustrated at the inequities and even more committed to making sure that that part of my work and that part of my life is designed to remove those inequities, because they impact everyone.

I've never wished that I wasn't black. I have wished that people were more insightful. I have wished that people were more compassionate. I've wished that other people could see me for the complex being that I am, not see past my race but see that and all of the things that I have done, to embrace all of me.

Okay, so maybe Cheryl is stronger than some of us. Meanwhile, my stand-up comic panelists both acknowledged that in their younger years, they contended with Denial of Blackness attacks but have since strongly embraced race as part of their identities:

W. KAMAU BELL

I think I spent the first seventeen years of my life probably not wanting to be black half the time, at least. It seemed hard from the perspective of being one of the few black kids in the private school. Then it seemed hard from the perspective of when I was around black people: they could smell that I hadn't been around black people.

And so I spent a lot of time not wanting to be black, just because it was like, "This is too much pressure from both sides."

It wasn't until probably I turned eighteen, I read The Autobiography of Malcolm X. *I started listening to the bands Living Color and Fishbone. And I found that, "Oh, there's different ways to be black? Oh, wait a minute. Oh, okay. I like these ways. Wait a minute, John Coltrane? I like these ways." And I started to assemble my own version of blackness.*

In my mind, I picture a nineteen-year-old Kamau at a special Toy Shoppe for Self-Determination. He browses the aisles and happens upon the object of his search: a very-special-edition LEGO™ Negro Identity Building Set. It comes with pieces of various shapes and sizes, and on the side of the box is printed:

> **Build the black identity that works for you! Tired of being pressured by black people and others to fit their idea of blackness? Don't wear the "right" clothes? Don't listen to the "right" music? Don't commit the "right" crimes? This set will liberate you. Inside you'll find every country, every type of food, every genre of film, all granting you the unlimited power to be whoever you want to be while maintaining your strong sense of blackness.**

ELON JAMES WHITE

When I was growing up I totally knew that it would be an easier world if I was white because then I wouldn't be yelled at by my uncle and my mother when we were in arguments about race.

I will fully admit that I didn't have the clear, strong feeling that I'm supposed to be black probably until the last couple of years when I realized that this time in history, what I do, the discussions I have, everything that I really find important is based on the idea that I feel that a people has been mistreated. And that even now, after all of the bullshit that happened, we're in this weird line of things where it's like well, we're not slaves, but we're not equal.

So I feel like I am supposed to be black now, and I would never want to change it now only because, as a random white guy, especially if I was a stand-up or something like that, I don't feel I could do as much good as being a black guy in this time making the arguments that I make.

Many black people reach a point of tension with their own black community when that community rejects their membership in Club Blackness and forces that person to make The Choice, as in the Questionably Black Person must choose either to continue the unauthorized activity or continue being black. This usually revolves around an activity that doesn't fit the community's cultural definition of blackness. Sometimes, sadly, it's achievement-based, such as an academic or extracurricular organization. Other times it's athletic, and can include a decision to pick a "non-black" sport over a "black" sport. Often it has nothing to do with what one does but rather *with whom* one is doing it.

JACQUETTA SZATHMARI

I had a best friend, Amanda Fry. She was white, and at a certain point when we were in third or fourth grade some black girls were like, "You have to choose between being friends with this white girl," who's my best friend since we were four and a half or five years old, "or all black people."

I was like, "Well, sorry, all black people. You lose out because this is my friend. I'm just going to be black on my own. I don't have time for that."

Those kinds of situations, over time, crop up in more subtle ways as you get older, of people trying to force you to make a choice. But it's a false dichotomy. You can never choose or not choose to be black. It's impossible. It's like choosing to be five foot one or not be five foot one.

While lots of black people have had the desire to escape their blackness, Christian spent a good part of his childhood wanting to escape his whiteness and trade it for anything else:

CHRISTIAN LANDER

I've been made fun of by my father all the time for wanting to be anything but white. I wanted to be black for a really long time. I wanted to be Asian for a really long time. I wanted to be anything but white, absolutely.

White culture is very bland and generic. There are no secrets to white culture; it's all out there. If you're white and you go into a fancy restaurant in Santa Monica, there's no secret menu, you're not going to get a white discount from the waiter.

[When you're not white], you get this extra, separate thing. You

get the culture of your family from somewhere else. You get this whole separate world. You get this amazing food and language and all of this stuff given to you.

As whites, believe me, we get plenty of privileges that make up for it, but I was always envious of that. I was so envious that you could be part of both.

Having a black-guy-born-in-Africa on The Black Panel gave me the chance to ask Derrick about specific instances in which he wanted to distance himself, not just from being black, but specifically from African-Americans.

DERRICK ASHONG

Are there ever any moments when I want to distance myself from Black America? Yeah, sometimes that happens. When I was in Boston, I was doing this hip-hop youth political-empowerment stuff, and the New Black Panther Party people came in, and they hit us with the "blacker than thou. We're blacker than all y'all, blacker than thou. Blah, blah, blah."

That doesn't really work with me, because I am African. You're never going to get me with the "blacker than thou." I'm just not feeling it.

I try not to be chauvinistic with it. I don't think Africans are superior or anything like that, but when people start to question my authentic blackness, I'm like, "I can trace my ancestry back forever in Africa. You can't really mess with me on that. I know my language, I know my culture, and I don't have to hate anyone in order to give myself an identity."

What happened in this instance is there was this idea among some of the New Black Panther Party people—not everybody, but some of the leadership—of "Kill Whitey. Kill white people."

DERRICK: Why?

NBPP: Oh, you have to kill Whitey. You know, the White Man this and this and this.

DERRICK: Well, first of all, I ain't really here to kill anybody. I'm in grad school. I'm trying to get a degree, do my thing. I came to do research. I don't know what you're talking about killing nobody for. Secondly, you ain't got a murder rap. You ain't killed nobody, either, as far as I know. You date mad white girls, so I don't exactly see what the beef is. And, additionally, when you say, "Kill Whitey," it just doesn't resonate with me. Because where I come from all the people who are oppressing us look like us.

NBPP: Yes, but the White Man and Colonialism, and this and this and this.

DERRICK: Yes, that's real. That's real. Colonialism happened. We got free. Colonialists do not dominate us the same way that they used to.

So when you say to an average kid in a place like Ghana, or anywhere in West Africa for sure, "We hate white people," it's like, "Well, why?" We have no proximate animus. We have no reason to dislike white folks.

When I was seeing that coming from this group of exclusively African-Americans who were explicitly Afrocentric, but had very little interest in an actual African perspective, it made me want to distance myself.

So for the most part I don't feel a strong sense to distance myself from African-American culture. But when it comes to making race the defining factor of everything, I just can't get with it. I can't get with it because ultimately you have to remember I have a responsibility to my people back home and race is not what's killing us. There are other issues in the world.

Can You Swim?

THERE ARE a number of persistent stereotypes about the things black people *don't* or *can't* do: eat organic food, tip, go camping, do yoga, travel, show up on time, et cetera.* Sometimes large portions of the black community embrace one or another of such notions, but in my own life, I actually tend to do and enjoy the things commonly on the list of activities black people don't do. I blame my mother. She got us started on organic food, yoga, travel, and more, very early on. One of the most persistent things black people allegedly don't do is swim, but there, too, my mom got me started early.

When I was six or seven years old, my mother enrolled me in swimming classes at one of the YMCAs in Washington, DC. The pool was the largest I had seen at that point in my life, but our

---

* For a more complete exploration of what black folk don't do, check out the Web video series at blackfolkdont.com.

class stuck to the very shallow end and took advantage of various tools and flotation devices for most of the weeks of the class. One day I showed up for what I expected to be another day of splashing around in my floaties when the teachers lined all of us up at the deep end of the pool. We had never been at that end before, and I was terrified. Then I discovered true terror when, one by one, the teachers told us to swim.

I complained loudly, "But you never taught us how!" They ignored my very reasonable protest and began flinging children into the depths. It was the Middle Passage all over again. Clearly, they were trying to kill us! I saw the first few children survive these attempted executions, but that had no effect on my fears about my own chances of survival. Surely, I thought, I was about to die at the hands of these heartless serial killers masquerading as YMCA swimming instructors.

When it was my turn to take the leap of the lemming, I stood at the edge of the pool a long time, reminding all who had ears to hear, that *I did not know how to swim because I had never been swimming before.* This was so obviously wrong. I searched the faces of others at the pool for any sign of sympathy, any acknowledgment of my agony, but all I got in return were smiles. Sick people, I thought. My blood was about to be on their hands. I cried, and just as I had set my mind to flee this crime scene, someone *pushed me into the pool.* My short life flashed before my eyes. I saw myself in the hospital a few years earlier, healing from third-degree burns to my left foot. I saw myself hating my first taste of beer courtesy of my pickup truck–driving father. I saw our dog, Honey, and knew I would miss her peculiar habit of playing with rocks instead of sticks.

"It's all over," I thought, as my body became completely

submerged in a pool far deeper than my young body's height. I panicked and flailed briefly, inhaling what felt like gallons of chlorinated water, and just as I resigned myself to death's cool embrace, a miracle happened. My body began to swim! I can't say *I* began to swim, because I didn't feel that the conscious *me* was in charge, but nevertheless, I was swimming. Everyone cheered, and when I emerged from the pool at the other end, exhausted but alive, one of the instructors boasted, "We *told* you you could do it!" And I thought, "No, you tried to kill me, but unfortunately for you, I just discovered a superpower."

After that traumatic introduction, I grew to love swimming in whatever body of water was nearest: oceans, rivers, lakes, and pools. I even spent a year on my high school swim team, though I found out that my body wasn't really constructed for competitive swimming. Today, in my constant travels, I always make sure to use the pool at whatever hotel I'm in. I consider the ability to swim a natural, fun, and important part of my life, and I'm still black. I threw this question of swimming ability to The Black Panel, and here's what they came back with.

CHRISTIAN LANDER

Can I swim? Yeah, absolutely. Just like any good white person, I took swimming lessons. I earned the badges all throughout my childhood. I had a pool at my house, which is weird because we were the only house in the neighborhood in downtown Toronto with a pool. It's probably the only reason I had as many friends as I had in high school. Yes, I can swim. I'm a pretty accomplished swimmer. I can do the butterfly.

JACQUETTA SZATHMARI

I love to swim, and I love water sports. I like water skiing. I like wind surfing. I used to do that when I was younger a lot. I grew up on the water. When you're from the Eastern Shore of Maryland— this used to infuriate me—[there were] free swimming lessons. Why was I the only black person, girl or boy, at my age that would take the free swimming lessons? Everyone else would just be like, "Brother at the pool! Ah!" afraid that water would get splashed up on their face. I'm like, "Who cares? We're all nappy-headed, shot to the grease. A little bit of water isn't going to hurt. It's free."

Plus, I'm OCD and very pragmatic, so I'm like, "If I fall in the water off a boat or something like that, I need to know what I'm doing." I don't know what it is about the swimming thing. I like to swim. It's good exercise.

ELON JAMES WHITE

Funny enough, I can't swim and it's not because I'm black. I went to summer camp as a child, and we used to go to the beach and stuff like that, there were chances to learn how to swim, I just didn't learn how to swim. I also can't drive. I live in New York!

DAMALI AYO

I am not a very good swimmer. I have control issues, so when my feet get too far off the ground, I panic. That might be a history of just distrust built in from the oppression, but it could be a childhood problem.

CHERYL CONTEE

I can swim. Actually, I took swimming lessons at the local suburban pool. My swimming, though, could be stronger. But yeah,

I can swim. That said, there were some interesting pool interactions with the local kids.

Our school was very, very white. Our neighborhood was very, very white. The pool was very, very white, and we came in for some bullying and some targeted, I would say, not very positive interactions.

I remember my brother, a kid asked him if his color would wash off, if that was going to be a problem for him. Another kid wanted to know why my [hands were different colors on the top and bottom]. Yeah.

DERRICK ASHONG

Yes, I can swim. I can swim quite well. I learned to swim relatively late.

You know what's funny? If I go to the beach, I ain't getting in the water. It's cold, and I like to be warm. I'm also not just going to sit around in the sun all the time, because I have a tan. So when I go to the beach, I walk around in the sand, I buy a hot dog, and I go home. If there's volleyball, we'll play it. Otherwise we sit, we look at the girls, and kick it. But I'm not into jumping around in the ocean overly much.

I can swim, though, and I used to play water polo in school and things like that. It was fun. I used to be on a swim team. I was always the last one, because my bones are dense.

W. KAMAU BELL

I can swim well. I've been swimming all my life. I'm a fairly good swimmer. Yes, I can swim. I can do several different strokes . . . I can't float that much, but that's because I'm 250 pounds, six foot four, built for slavery and the revolution.

Going Black to Africa

I **N ADDITION** to not being able to swim, black people also allegedly don't travel, but I traveled a lot during my childhood. My
mother thought it was essential to mix things up, and we were
constantly taking economically efficient road trips in our Nis-
san Datsun B210 station wagon. She loved that car and wielded
it almost as if it were a part of her body. By the time I graduated from high school, we had traveled from Nova Scotia, Canada, to Disney World in it. I can only recall one plane journey in
my childhood, but we moved about by Amtrak train quite often.
When I was twelve, we took a nearly three-week train trip around
the entire United States and deep into Mexico. In many of the
places we visited, we chose highly efficient, low-carbon-footprint
accommodations, also known as "camping."

The Mexico part of that epic train journey was a trip itself.
I met travel writers in Los Mochis, saw forest fires from our bus
on the Mexican highway near the U.S.-Mexico border, and heard

country music blasting out of a car stereo for the first time in my life. I didn't know it was even possible to blast country music! I'm not sure I thought it wasn't possible. I just know the thought had never crossed my mind before that day. I've been a changed man ever since.

All these trips, however, paled in comparison to the journey I was privileged enough to take to Senegal in the summer of 1995, just after graduating high school.

One of the French teachers at Sidwell had established a ritual of taking his students to France every summer. Joining one of these trips never concerned me since (a) I was a Spanish student, and (b) they cost a serious amount of money. My senior year, however, word spread that Monsieur Gueye[*] was not going to France that summer, but to his home country of Senegal. This got the attention of every black person associated with Sidwell, and the opportunity was the daily focus of attention in the Thurston household for months until I boarded the plane.

For me, bearing an African name, having matriculated through a West African–inspired rites-of-passage program, and being my mother's son, going on this trip was no choice at all. It was a duty. My mother was especially excited to go but couldn't afford to send us both, so I represented the entire family: myself, my sister, my mother, and those who came before but never got to return. I was honored, humbled, and excited! I read as much as I could in the library[†] and planned my packing list. We were

---

[*] His first name is Mamadou, but young people do not call African elders by their first names. If you are under forty-five years old, he is "Monsieur Gueye"!

[†] This was pre-Google!

told that bartering was a major form of commerce and U.S. goods could fetch a good price, so I rummaged through my clothing, toys, and other possessions identifying anything dispensable.

This was also my first foreign travel to a country that required a passport, and in the process of applying we discovered a *small* technical problem: my name wasn't actually Baratunde Rafiq Thurston, not legally at least. I never knew there was any issue with my name before this. As a kid, you just accept what your mother tells you, with no concern for or awareness of "paperwork" and "laws."

But all official records still had me with my father's surname, making me Baratunde Rafiq Robinson. That just sounds so strange to me, even now. It doesn't sound like me, and it isn't. My mother located a DC lawyer to help her quickly file for an official name change based on the extensive paper trail of school records, communion documents, and other reports demonstrating that I was known as "Baratunde Thurston." Miraculously, we were able to get me a passport with the Thurston name in time for the trip. A few vaccinations later, I was off to The Source Code of Blackness.

On July 25, 1995, our group met at National Airport—I still refuse to call it Reagan Airport; National for life!—and we took group photos and hugged the family members we were leaving behind. The girls on the trip had dressed up slightly, wearing nice shorts or slacks and solid-color tops. The guys dressed like we were going to just kick it on the stoop, as usual. We rocked oversize white Ts, baseball caps, and Timberland boots. After a quick hop to JFK Airport, we boarded Air Afrique and flew to the east, my brother to the east, my brother to the east, my brother to the east . . .

. . .

I'M NOT SURE JUST what I expected. Would there be a version of the Walmart greeter but specifically for black Americans on a roots-discovering pilgrimage? "Welcome home, brother! We have waited many years for your return! Your African name is . . ." Would there be some version of the Hollywood Walk of Fame, still-wet concrete into which we would dip our hands and feet to prove we had made the return trip? Would there be a special place in the mountains, surrounded by all the creatures of the mother continent bowing their heads in respectful celebration, and behind them a fountain from which pure, pristine, unadulterated blackness flowed?

Wow, that's not a bad idea. African nations seeking to boost tourism could probably convince at least a few American blacks that The Fountain of Blackness existed within their borders. Certainly a part of me, and perhaps all of us on the journey, was looking for something: a more tangible connection to our ancestry; a validation of our Afrocentricity; something to justify the investment in red, black, and green medallions and Black Power fists. We at least wanted some good deals on kente cloth!

Monsieur Gueye had arranged for us to stay at a downtown Dakar Sofitel Hotel with views of the city and the ocean beyond. The hotel was clean and just what you'd expect from any modern urban lodging. What I did not expect to find was a previously unheard-of flavor of CNN, called CNN International. It was like the CNN in the United States, but they seemed to engage in this peculiar activity known as "reporting" and were less focused on distracting the viewer with swooshy graphics. Don't worry. CNN International isn't easily available in the States.

We rolled around much of the capital by bus. I took photos and referred to them as "drive-by shootings," because living in an actual crack-inspired DC war zone led me to believe this was funny.

Shot:

An armed guard stands at attention, his hands clasped behind his back and his automatic rifle slung across his chest. His uniform is a red, buttoned-up military jacket and red cap embroidered with a golden ring of fabric, plus jet-black pants, complemented by an expressionless jet-black face. Behind him lies the large, white presidential palace, separated from this black man with black pants and black gun by a wrought-iron black fence.

Shot:

Three young boys wave to us as our bus passes along an ocean-side road. They are each wearing pants of a different color: one red, one white, one blue.

Shot:

A group of women heats a large pot of water over a man-made outdoor fire. Whether their purpose is to cook food or launder clothes, I cannot tell.

Shot:

Three men sit against the wall on the edge of an outdoor market. The one nearest us exhales a piercingly lovely wail through his saxophone. Next to him a man seated on the ground strikes his mallet against the wooden bars of a xylophone. The third man plucks notes from his string instrument.

The bus stopped.

We had to hit up the small, partially indoor market crammed between two buildings on the side of the road. Parents, siblings, and distant relatives would have sent us the thousands of miles back if we didn't return with some "authentic piece of Africa" for them. We spent most of our time in the market looking at "sand paintings," which are made from a variety of different-colored sands from across the continent to create imagery indistinguishable from non-sand paintings at a far enough distance. I froze when I saw this painted in sand:

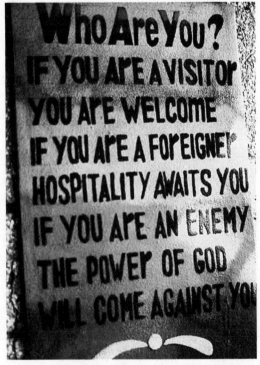

The sand painting that purported to welcome people.

Dang! Senegalese folk have some mad dramatic welcome art! In the U.S. we just print WELCOME on a mat, and leave it outside our front door. West Africans invoke the wrath of God. I saw that painting, and was like, "I'm a *foreigner* and a *visitor*. I am *not* an enemy. I repeat. *Foreign. Visitor.*"

Shot:
My schoolmate Chip sits in the foreground. He's wearing a polo shirt and has a video camera hanging around his neck. We are on a boat. In the background is Goree Island.

Goree Island was the final point of departure for many slaves headed to the Americas and was our next major stop on the trip. Monsieur Gueye had arranged for a guided tour of the compound where wave after wave of captive Africans were housed, processed, and shipped westward across the Atlantic, if not from this exact location, then from others like it along the western coast of the continent.

Walking in the centuries-old footsteps of ancestors is probably the most humbling thing I've experienced in my life. We stood in the cramped cells. We held the weighted shackles. We looked through the infamous doorway of no return that opens directly onto the ocean and offered a one-way ticket to the afterlife for troublemaking captives. At low tide, people fell to a rocky death. At high tide, sharks, accustomed to fresh meals, awaited the occasional plunge.

This was, by far, the quietest portion of our trip. No jokes. No enthusiasm. Silence that sounded like what it was: our awe and respect.

Shot:

Our teacher, Monsieur Gueye, stands under a tree that towers above him. When he was a child he planted this tree.

One of the most enjoyable and shocking parts of the trip was our visit to Monsieur Gueye's village. The adults with us joined the village elders and talked about adult things.

We students hung out with some of the kids there, who took us on a long walk. They all commented on our appearance: "You look so old!" they kept saying to us. Apparently, for our ages, we black American kids had a Benjamin Button thing going on. We joked among ourselves that America had caused us to suffer from racism-induced early aging. After the village tour, it was time for the meal, which is always the highlight of any of my trips.

I remember one of the women of the village "introducing" us to a live chicken. He was really cute. Then she told us we had just met our dinner. I was fine with that. To this day, I count that meal of extremely fresh chicken and couscous as one of the top five meals of my life. I loved it so much I took a picture of it. I was foodspotting in 1995!

Our Senegalese journey ended with a visit to two extremely different places. The first was a resort on the coast. Again, our teacher wanted to provide us with a range of impressions. The resort was hot (physically and metaphorically). I got really excited when I found out there were nude beaches nearby, but then very unexcited when I saw it was heavily populated by fat, naked Germans. That was not the image I wanted of the Motherland.

One of the best meals of my life, foodspotted in 1995.

The last significant stop we made was a cultural center built in honor of Senegal's first president, Léopold Sédar Senghor. Senghor was the man. A noted writer, poet, cultural theorist, and politician, as we learned on the tour, he was the only African admitted to the vaunted Académie Française, a French institution that has existed for centuries as the authority on the French language. Senghor is also well known for creating the cultural-historical concept of Negritude, which sought to elevate the cultural history of Africa to the same level as that of Europe. In his own way, perhaps Senghor was living the tenets of a book we'd call *How to Be African*.

The trip had more than met my expectations. I did buy a crapload of kente cloth at amazing prices. I ate local foods. I purchased "African art." I returned to a site of the trans-Atlantic slave trade. I dodged aggressive street vendors who were so persistent as to follow us for a *mile*. But the absolute moment of magic occurred while my friends and I were swimming in the Atlantic Ocean.

The waves were smooth and massive. I was in Africa looking west back to America, and I thought to myself, "I could die now, and be so very happy." It wasn't that I had a desire to die. What I felt, though, was a sense of completion, satisfaction, and contentedness I'd never known before that moment. Making that journey did not make me any blacker, but it completed a circle in my life that I hadn't realized was broken until it was made whole again.

But I Don't Want to Kill People

The reason why people send their kids to a place like Sidwell is to get them into a place like Yale.

—*Cheryl Contee*

I'VE ALWAYS loved talking to people, asking them questions and researching options. From the time I was in elementary school, my mother began tasking me with all family phone-based research. Whether we were planning a vacation, searching for a gutter-cleaning service, or looking for just the right pair of Ma's cowboy boots, it was my job to call around and get the best deal. I was absolutely *made* for the college-search experience, and I especially loved college fairs.

Unlike in my phone research, I could interrogate these college representatives in person and collect the shiny brochures full of idyllic photos that make each campus look like a retirement home for young adults where everyone plays sports, everyone reads outside, and everyone is happy. There was never a question about whether or not I was going to go to college. Sidwell's tuition was an investment in improved college prospects, and I was not about to waste it. But, as sophomore year and standardized testing season began, I didn't have very strong ideas about where to apply. I just knew that cost and financial aid were going to be important.

I'd almost had to leave Sidwell for financial reasons after my freshman year, and convinced my mother to keep me there only after extensive lobbying. I sold her hard on my desire to stay there, explaining that I'd just been elected as vice president of the Black Student Union, was doing well in classes, and all my friends were there. Meanwhile, I made a bold and persuasive case directly to the school's development and financial aid office, explaining that I might have to leave because of money and asking them to increase my grants. I figured it would be a loss for both of us if I had to drop out for financial reasons. They looked good on my résumé, and I looked good on theirs! That experience taught me that sometimes the best way to get something is simply to make your case and directly ask for it. You might just get the affirmative answer you're looking for.

Most significant, I made a deal with my mother: she would continue to cover the cost of Sidwell, and I would be responsible for covering the cost of college. I readily agreed to take on that debt burden. It was easy to do at sixteen years old. I had no idea how much college tuition was or that it would increase at over three times the rate of inflation.[*] Like the U.S. government, I figured I'd have a way to get the money when it came time to pay up, but for my high school self, this deal meant that in addition to

---

[*] It's true. Google it.

attending college fairs and information sessions, I attended special *scholarship* fairs and did independent research on every possible way to pay for school. At one scholarship fair, I had an unforgettable encounter with a man from the navy.

I never had any intention of going into the navy or any other branch of the armed services. I was a hyperpolitical, self-righteous, semimilitant kid who attended a Quaker school, railed against U.S. imperialism and "no blood for oil," and remembered proudly and loudly that black folks had refused the Vietnam draft. As I was walking by the navy booth on my way to some non-military destination, a bald black man in uniform tried to sell me on the navy and how much it would pay and all the great leadership and technical skills I would acquire with its money. I had to cut him off.

"I'm sorry. I'm not really interested," I said.

"Why not?"

"I don't want to kill people."

"Oh, you don't have to kill people! You can work on the mechanical side."

"But then I'd be helping fix machines that people use to kill people, so basically I'll be killing people, and I don't want to kill people."

"Okay, but you could work in our technology division. Satellites! Radar! Networks! All the cool stuff."

"Right, but once again all that cool stuff is in the service of killing people, which I already told you I don't want to do."

We were at an impasse. He was trying to convince me that the navy had all this great opportunity and money to cover my college costs. I was trying to convince him that murder wasn't really my thing. The man became frustrated and called in reinforcements in the form of an older white man drenched in medals (probably for killing people). The Decorated One warmed up:

"So I understand you have some hesitation about applying for a navy scholarship," he said confidently.

"No, no hesitation at all. I'm *definitely* not interested. As I told your colleague here, *I don't want to kill people*." Did the black dude think that a white man would be more effective at getting me to compromise my non-murder values? I stuck to my guns, and eventually both men moved on to other prospects.

By my junior year at Sidwell, when it was actually time to apply, I had developed a little more clarity around my college goals, and the last place I imagined I would end up was a New England liberal arts school. I had recently read Andrew Hacker's book *Two Nations*, which chronicles persistent racial and class segregation in America. According to Hacker, some of the whitest states in the U.S. at the time were in New England. The idea of committing myself to this region for four years freaked me out, but my fears weren't only over race. I had become obsessed with the region's notorious coastal and air pollution—I was also a little environmentalist—and I imagined stranded whales rotting on a litter-strewn, segregated beach patrolled by racist cops and owned by preppy frat boys who beat black kids like me with their lacrosse sticks. The End Times, basically.

Even beyond the issues of race and flesh-dissolving oceans, attending a New England liberal arts college felt redundant. Part of the reasoning behind attendance at such schools is to prepare yourself for mainstream society and figure out how to "play the game," especially as a black person in America. I thought six years at Sidwell had already accomplished that. I had become comfortable among the upper class and the powerful. I went to parties in Potomac, Maryland. I got a part-time job at the *Washington Post*, due to a Sidwell connection. Chelsea Clinton signed my yearbook! I became an inside man.

Most important, my big lessons from Sidwell weren't *all* dark and oppressive and horrific. On the contrary, I made great friends and received a great education. The teachers there pushed my mind much harder than I'd been used to, and the resources I was able to exploit there are the foundation for most of what I've made of my life. Those resources included early access to the Internet (1993!), impressive science labs, a real focus on writing, and the general idea of entitlement. By "entitlement," I don't mean "What's mine is mine, and what's yours is mine!" I mean the sense of personal possibility. It's places like Sidwell that produce people who feel that they can do anything they want, and that the world is their playground. Their (our) default orientation is "Yes, we can."

Still, all the acclimation had exhausted this brother, and I was pretty sure I'd had about enough of white people, at least for a while. I'd learned valuable lessons and was ready to go home.

In my mind, home was a historically black college, specifically Morehouse College in Atlanta. The older brother of one of my best friends had graduated from Sidwell and pursued a combined engineering degree program from Morehouse and Georgia Tech. I saw his path and wanted to walk in his exact footsteps. That would have been physically difficult, since I stand at about five feet nine inches, and he's over six feet, but metaphorically speaking, I saw his path as my future.

I looked forward to a college life in which I didn't feel the constant need to defend or speak for my entire race. I figured a black college would offer me that. Then my friend Paul, two years older and attending Harvard, sent me an e-mail that changed my life. I've since lost the original, but the gist of his message was, "You really need to check out Harvard. I'm having a great time, and I think you'd like it here."

Paul is one of those guys for whom I have extreme respect. We had spent ridiculous hours together working on the high school newspaper, *Horizon*, and when you regularly work with someone until four a.m., you either discover that they're one of the best people you know, or you begin plotting ways to make them disappear. With Paul, it was the former. My mother loved Paul, too, so his opinion went a long way in our household. Shortly after his e-mail, I attended a Harvard information session at Sidwell early one weekday morning. I was shocked by the appearance of the man running the session. He was black, short, partially bald, and immaculately dressed in a suit, white shirt, and bow tie. My first thought was, "A Black Muslim is in charge of Harvard recruiting? Where's the bean pie!?" The man, of course, was not a member of the Nation of Islam. His name was David Evans, and he was (and still is) a senior admissions officer for Harvard College. He's responsible for much of the significant boost in the enrollment of minority students at Harvard since the early 1970s and has been honored numerous times in recent years for his contributions. I don't remember anything specific that he said during that high school information session—I think I was too distracted by the bow tie—but his presence was unforgettable, and the fact that he was at Sidwell representing Harvard left a massive impression on me.

With Paul's recommendation and the bean pie–less, bow-tied

admissions officer on my mind, we added Harvard to the Summer Thurston Family College Tour 1994 (STFCT 1994!! Woohoo!!!).

Like our camping trips of yore, we loaded up the family vehicle, an Isuzu Trooper at this point, with the essentials: AAA map books, peanut butter, books on tape, and the family dog, Honey. There was no such thing as a Thurston family road trip without the dog, and her opinion probably counted as much as my own in the college-planning process.

This tour reminded me of my visits to DC private schools six years prior, and I had as many instant judgments this time around.

I don't remember much of Yale besides the physical darkness. I found the Gothic architecture a little frightening, and the city of New Haven felt like an afterthought compared to the school's campus. The whole place made me feel gloomy, and I couldn't get past it.

The idea of MIT was a natural fit in some ways. I was a big math and science nerd and figured I would end up working in math or computer science as a profession. MIT is a school that refers to its buildings by numbers, which I thought was cool, but it was also trying too hard to convince us that there were "women" and "fun" available there. The tour hosts actually showed us a video talking only about how much fun students at MIT have. The school doth protest too much, I thought, but once I actually became a student at Harvard, I was surprised to discover that MIT did indeed know how to party and certainly black MIT was the hub of much of black Harvard's social life.

My mother and I tried to visit Northeastern University but couldn't find it for the longest time. In the search process, we came across the intersection of Tremont Street and Tremont Street. I'm not kidding. If you wonder why Boston drivers are so famously terrible, consider that they have to navigate space-time paradoxes like this, and cut them some slack.

Harvard, contrary to these other experiences, just felt right.

My tour leader was named Peter, and he was a member of something called the Crimson Key Society. After I enrolled, I determined that these student volunteers are disturbingly enthusiastic and love Harvard a little too much. They smile *all* the time. They have little anecdotes about *everything*. I don't think they are capable of expressing anger. If you are ever in Cambridge, Massachusetts, you should test this out by doing your best to annoy them. They're unbreakable. But on my first-ever visit to campus, I actually found Peter's excitement exciting.

Cambridge was beautiful, and so was the school's campus. People were playing sports and reading outside, and just like in the brochures, *everyone* looked happy. That tour affected me for reasons other than the pleasing appearance, though. I also got this inexplicable feeling that this was a place I could be myself.

My mom and our dog, Honey, had not joined me for the tour. They were posted in the Cambridge Common, a triangle-shaped park at the center of Harvard Square where, in 1775, George Washington first gathered a group of volunteer fighters that would become the U.S. Army. In her own stories of how I ended up at Harvard, my mother would always recount how she saw me returning to them in the park: "You were floating, and I knew it. This boy wants to go to Harvard!"

Being Black at Harvard

NO ONE said hello.

The day I moved into my freshman dorm in Harvard Yard began early that morning in a room at the Susse Chalet motel three miles north of Harvard Square. My mother, our dog, Honey, and our Isuzu Trooper arose in the modest accommodations, like on so many previous Thurston Family road trips. My mother boiled water for tea in her portable hot pot. I walked the dog. But there was more excitement on this day. Moving into your freshman college dorm is an exciting time. The kids are moments away from being able to do whatever they want with whomever they want. For parents, it's the same: "Get out of my house, you freeloader. I want to invite some friends over and drink without having to worry about you ruining it." In my memory, the actual act of moving in is replayed in slow motion, like a car crash. But to this day, beyond the visual impression of station wagons, footlockers, and hugs, most of what I remember is that no one in town or on campus looked me in the eye or said hello as they passed.

I wondered if it was just me, but my mother noticed the same thing, and we were dressed well enough, didn't smell, and were friendly folks. Where we came from, you greeted people, but that wasn't the case in the Boston area.

Beyond a general coldness, Boston can be especially unfriendly for black people. There's a rich and beautiful history of black people in Boston from the days of abolition to the Civil Rights Movement and beyond, but recent history has overshadowed much of that.

Today, there's a significant black community in Boston but relatively little in the way of black political or economic power, and of course as rich as the history is, it's also plagued by ugliness. The Red Sox were the last Major League baseball team to integrate and chose to pass on Jackie Robinson in the 1940s. During the wave of forced busing and school integration in the 1970s, Boston stood out for its violent reaction, and the image of a white Bostonian wielding an American flag as a weapon, aiming it at a black man as if ready to impale him, has never left my head.

On an average visit to Boston, unless you know where to go, you don't see the diversity in public that exists in other major U.S. cities and in Boston itself.* Never before have I been to an American city that so effectively hides its black population, and I lived there for twelve years. It's as if the Underground Railroad were

---

* Recent census data reveal that Boston is just under 50 percent white. No one told the city!

still active! All of this supports my conclusion that people in Boston generally are not friendly to outsiders, and I found this to be the case on my first day as a resident, even in the friendlier, more liberal town across the Charles River, mockingly referred to as "The People's Republic of Cambridge."

When someone finally did break the pattern by smiling and greeting us, my mother exclaimed, "Oh, thank you so much for saying hello!" This reasonable and well-home-trained person was a fellow freshman in my dorm, and she was black.

I didn't know much about my roommate before arriving. I knew, like me, he had a unique name, Dahni-El (pronounced *donny*-el), grew up in Brooklyn, and had attended a New England boarding school. When I opened the door to our room, he had already moved in. The first thing I saw was a footlocker covered in a large red, black, and green flag. I thought to myself, "We are going to be the most militant-looking brothers on this campus!" Between his Afrocentric flag, my fresh-back-from-Africa kente clothing, and our names, I imagined our room would be the hub of the black Harvard revolution. We would convene late at night and strategize by candlelight over heavily marked maps with zones flagged "The Man" and "The People." It would be great.

After the initial image of Afrocentric blackness, Dahni-El and I discovered that we also shared a general lack of financial resources. Neither of us owned a television,* so one of our neighbors used crayons to draw a picture of a television and taped it to

---

* I did own a boom box with a four-inch black-and-white TV screen, but that really doesn't count.

the wall where she thought the real thing should have been. We left it there all year. To help cover our tuition and expenses, we both held campus jobs in a department called Dorm Crew. That meant cleaning hallways and stairways, removing trash from dorms, and scrubbing bathrooms inside student residences. Yes, we performed your basic janitorial duties, because it was one of the highest-paying jobs on campus. Its high wages meant Dorm Crew attracted financial aid recipients,* and a disproportionate number of workers were minorities.

I think I know what you're thinking: "Baratunde, are you telling me that poor black kids at Harvard literally cleaned up the shit of their fellow Harvard students?" To answer you, I would clarify that it wasn't only black kids, and we cleaned much more than shit. Bathrooms are diverse ecosystems, requiring the cleaning up of hair, toothpaste, and soap scum. It's an admittedly strange dynamic, but it came with amazing privileges, and you would be hard-pressed to find a stronger advocate of the Dorm Crew program than me.

In the beginning, the arrangement is awkward for the cleaner and the cleanee. Imagine answering your dorm's buzzer to find your chemistry lab partner standing there with a bucket of cleaning supplies and a mop, demanding access to your bathroom. But

---

* Shortly after I graduated from Harvard in 1999, the competition among Ivy League schools for new students increased drastically. Princeton led the way by offering full-ride scholarships to academically qualified students who met a certain financial threshold. Harvard and others followed suit. My understanding now is that working a campus job is far less common than it was during my time there. This, of course, upsets me, because I had to clean shit when I went to Harvard, and kids these days don't know the value of work, and society is going to— Oh my goodness. I'm officially old.

it's something you get used to, and I relished not just the money but also the opportunity to escape the fast-paced world of ideas, debates, meetings, egos, papers, and the overall social noise of college and replace it with some solitary time scrubbing shower stalls. Dorm Crew was the least stressful part of my Harvard experience, providing much-needed downtime. Instead of thinking about my classes and assignments, I always carried a Walkman and either listened to books on tape (a habit I inherited from my mother) or conservative talk radio hosts Dr. Laura Schlessinger and Howie Carr. I didn't grow up listening to conservative arguments—my mother loved me—but I found it oddly comforting to broaden my political ideology inputs while breathing in large amounts of cleaning chemicals.

Dorm Crew wasn't just a dirty, well-paying job that offered mental escape. It was also a gateway to coveted jobs during Harvard's class reunions each spring. Few places welcome alumni back like Harvard. The premise of the reunion weekend is to remind people how great Harvard is, how much fun they had (even if they didn't), get them drunk, and get them to give money to Harvard so the cycle can repeat itself for the next generation. Through Dorm Crew, I performed a critical function in this process. I ran the liquor operations.

In order to hire students to work in various reunion jobs, the alumni office relies on Dorm Crew as a primary recruiting and filtering tool. People who climb the ranks and become Dorm Crew captains, with responsibility for scheduling, managing, and assessing multiple workers across an entire dorm during the school year, get the most sought-after jobs during reunion. Since your reunion clientele is comprised of twenty-six- to ninety-plus-year-old Harvard alumni who run a large slice of the world, there's an amazing opportunity to earn a significant pile of cash through tips. During my time at Harvard, four major categories of competitive reunion jobs were available: *Al Powers*, a logistics crew, which sets up tables, chairs, and tents for the various events; *Linen Crew*, which prepares dorm rooms for alumni to live in again as if they were young; *Bellhops*, who carry luggage and drive alumni around town; and *Liquor Crew*, which manages the procurement and distribution of all beer, wine, spirits, and other beverages.

There are many important jobs at Harvard University: the president, the heads of academic departments, deans, real estate directors, and the executives who manage the Harvard endowment. But Liquor Crew is *the most important job at Harvard* because it makes all other elements of Harvard possible, and for a time I ran it. My very first year, I worked as a bar back, serving non-mixed drinks and restocking ice, making sure cups and napkins were available, and generally being a grunt. It was because of this job that I first consciously became aware of how many hours are in a week: 168. Because the job paid an hourly wage, and because it only lasted for one week of the year, the goal was to work as many hours as possible, regardless of the effect on one's body. I worked over 100 hours that week. I learned how to rapidly set up and tear down a bar several times a day whether inside a two-hundred-year-old dining hall or in the middle of a football field. And I learned that no matter the time of day, there's some class of Harvard alumni ready to drink, from Bloody Marys in the morning for older alumni to cup after cup of beer for the younger reunion attendees.

The job was thrilling, chaotic, and entertaining, offering crash courses in supply-chain management and interpersonal communication. It also taught me that serving alcohol to alumni is the best way to understand the value of a Harvard education. I got the opportunity, time and again, to interact with people at every stage of post-college life. I saw their hormones on a rampage at the fifth-year reunion, their parenting skills under pressure at the fifteenth, their hairlines receding at an inverse rate to their income for the twenty-fifth, and their dwindling numbers beyond the fortieth. I spoke to and learned from all of these people, and the lesson was consistent and simple: "What you study here doesn't matter. Pursue your passion, and you'll figure out a way to earn a living at it down the line. Be yourself." Sometimes I received this lesson from people who had failed to apply it to themselves. Other times, it was clear they were living their dreams and proving their own point by example.

Not all of my Liquor Crew alumni interactions were so high-minded and positive, though. Many of these alumni attended Harvard at a time when people who looked like me cleaned their bathrooms, not as a campus job but as a lifetime career. The clash of generations and cultures could be intense, like the time a very old white man accused me of lying to him.

It happened during a reunion event for one of the older classes and took place at Eliot House, a dorm along the Charles River. We set up the bar on a terrace under a shining white tent. A string quartet played off to the side, setting an elegant mood. The bar was slammed with throngs of alumni, and my job was to keep the universe intact by serving as many of them as I could as quickly as possible. I felt like I was deployed with a MASH unit in a war zone. Ice was flying. The ground was slick, covered in

an alcoholic sludge. Knives and corkscrews were scattered across
the tables, providing a dangerous obstacle for fast-moving hands.
Knowing who had asked for what and in what order was impossible to keep straight. There was no line, no numbered ticket-
ing. There was pure adrenaline, instinct honed by training, and
chaos, out of which a lone voice managed to commandeer my
attention.

"Young man, you served *three* old people before me," a very
tall, very pale, white-haired man shouted at me.

"I'm sorry, sir. It's really busy. I didn't see you there. What can
I get for you?" I offered, with an apologetic smile.

"You're a *liar!*"

I turned to face this amazing charge, and his finger was in my
face, pointing at me and shaking. He yelled again with even more
vehemence, "You're a *liar!*"

This was no normal yell. I *heard* the words with my ears but I
also *felt* them in my soul. There was such anger and contempt in
his tone that I froze. It felt as if the voices of his incredulous ancestors were also yelling at me for daring even to be present.

I apologized again, and he responded by *threatening to have
my financial aid pulled*! At this point, someone else came over to
calm the lunatic down, but in that moment, I felt extraordinarily
black and angry and embarrassed.

Moments like these were rare. With all that I knew of the
world intellectually, with all that my mother had taught me, and
with all I had experienced firsthand at Sidwell, I was well prepared for, but rarely encountered, such raw ugliness. There was
an incident in which someone scrawled the word "nigger" on the
walls of my freshman dorm, and while it was painful, to me it also

felt a bit like old news. In the wake of *The Bell Curve,* a book that tried to intellectually support the idea of black people's native inferiority, Harvard professor Harvey Mansfield provoked a reaction by claiming most black students at Harvard were unqualified and only enrolled because of affirmative action. Again, incidents like these didn't make me feel great, but "intellectuals" and leaders and all sorts of people have been claiming black people's inferiority for centuries. I wasn't about to let their ignorance completely define my experience.

More often, my experience of race at Harvard was full of joy and excitement.

The Class of 1999 had a special bond. Not only did Prince personally write a song about us *and us alone,* we just came together quickly and well. This class cohesion crossed racial lines, but it was especially strong among the black students in my class. We regularly erupted into self-congratulatory chants of "Nine nine! Nine nine! Nine nine!" with absolutely no prompting. We were as likely to explode into cheers at a sporting event as in the dining hall or crossing the quad. The fact that it annoyed other classes was proof to us that we were right. "They're just jealous because they don't love themselves as much as we do, because we're clearly more awesome," we thought. We roamed the campus and the city, a sprawling swarm of self-love and blackness. One moment we were taking part in impromptu "Black Olympics" in Harvard Yard. The next moment we were taking over a weekend dance party in one of the upper-class houses. In one unforgettable event, we decided to go to the movies to see the film *Dead Presidents* starring Larenz Tate, Chris Tucker, and many more. Our Swarm of Blackness flooded the sidewalks and T station and subway cars, and as we crossed a bridge nearing the movie theater, we broke out into a run, descending the hill like Gandalf and the Rohirrim on the fifth day of battle at Helm's Deep in the *Lord of the Rings* movie. It was beautiful.

Yet for as much as I bonded with my black classmates and happily joined in the swarm, I also forged my own path based on interests that had nothing to do with race, and chief among these was technology.

My other campus job—I had several—was as a computer "user assistant," offering technical support in the campus computer labs and to students in their rooms. I worked my way up to the advanced support team, which was basically a tech support SWAT team. When all others failed, they would call us in to solve the problem. To this day, I still get Facebook messages from college classmates asking me for computer support. I also worked a job as a software tester and was active in the Harvard Computer Society, leading its tenth-anniversary book project. But the activity that consumed the largest share of my time was the *Harvard Crimson*, the school's paper.

Back in high school, I had discovered a deep love for and addiction to both the consumption and creation of news. I worked part-time as a copy aide at the *Washington Post*, was an editor on the school paper, and devoured news in print, and on radio and television. The Washington Association of Black Journalists offered a weekend journalism program that I enrolled in, which bolstered my interest in the field and led me deeper into the world. We even got to visit the press briefing room at the White House, an opportunity I used to get a photo of myself behind the podium striking a revolutionary pose, naturally.

Presitunde.

When I told Ken Cooper, the then-director of the program and former national editor for the *Boston Globe*, that I was going to Harvard, he didn't hesitate: "Do the *Crimson*," he said. I took his advice, and it was one of the best decisions I've made in my life.

The *Crimson* is a legendary institution. The daily has been around since 1873, is run by undergraduates with no oversight from the university, and claims some impressive alumni like Franklin Delano Roosevelt, the technology investor and philanthropist Esther Dyson, and CNBC's Jim Cramer (sorry!). The process of joining the staff is known as the "comp," and generally people choose one department to comp: news, photography, graphics, et cetera. I couldn't decide, so I went with news *and* photography. Over my years at the paper, I had a chance to cover a wide swath of campus activity, from student protests to the dean's office to science and technology policy. Merging my technology interests with the paper, I became cochair (with Jennifer 8. Lee) of the first ever "online" department in the paper's history. What I especially relished was the opportunity to have input into the staff editorial, the paper's official position on affairs of the day. Sunday nights, I got to experience directly how diversity in media could affect what the paper published, through the mentorship of an older black student and executive on the editorial board named Dave.

In one of the first meetings of the Black Students Association I ever attended, older classmates warned us, "Don't talk to the *Crimson*. They're racist!" A series of incidents that had occurred before the arrival of The Nine Nine had led to a total collapse of the relationship between the paper and black student leadership. The advice I got was not only to avoid talking to the paper but also avoid working there. As a budding newspaperman, my missing the chance to work on one of the top college newspapers in the nation wasn't an option. Enter Dave. We would often be the only black voices in the room when *Crimson* staff opinions were being debated, and I saw how he dropped in bits of perspective and knowledge, strongly advocated for certain positions, and often shifted the entire room. By engaging internally, Dave showed me an approach completely opposite of what I'd been told by some of the BSA leadership. The next year, Dave and I made a joint presentation to BSA members, encouraging them to join the paper, not just to affect the politics but also to take advantage of the ridiculous opportunities the place offered. If nothing else, it hosted some pretty sweet parties and was one of the few buildings on campus at the time to have a solidly working television.

Sure, race absolutely played a role in my Harvard experiences, whether friendships, political events, or other. But in general, the beauty of my Harvard experience is that I could often just be a student without having to actively and continuously think of myself as a *black* student. Upon graduation, I was conscious of the fact that I could be me and thus be black but not have to be black in order to be me.

Upon receiving my Harvard degree, an overwhelmingly proud mama embraced me on behalf of her efforts and the efforts of those who came before, exclaiming, "We did it!"

How to Be The Black Employee

WHEN I graduated from Harvard, I considered three basic employment paths: journalism, grad school, and some combination of technology and business. Despite my intense devotion to the *Harvard Crimson*, my journalistic career path was derailed the summer before my senior year when I had to bail on an internship at the *Washington Post* due to repetitive strain injury, commonly referred to at the time as carpal tunnel syndrome. Basically, I had gone hog-wild with overtyping on all the campus computer and Internet resources, and my wrists stopped working. I couldn't type, write, carry a lunch tray, or turn a doorknob without excruciating pain, so that summer, I chose instead to do a summer theatre program. In terms of grad school, I looked at a few options, but there was no particular academic problem I felt so passionately about that I wanted to stay in a university setting. I was ready to get out! Plus, it was 1999, and Internet-related anything was hot. Kids were getting venture-capital money for adding the word

"Web" to almost any idea, and the tech geek in me wanted to be close to that world, so, long before I worked full-time in writing and comedy, I took a job with a strategy consulting firm in Boston that focused on telecommunications, media, and Internet-related business.

It's hard to define what "strategy consulting" means to people who don't already know. Essentially, there is a category of professional business services offering "analysis" and "advice" and "strategy" to businesses that actually make and do real things. My role, especially in the beginning, was to conduct research related to ongoing projects and become a ninja with quantitative analysis and storytelling, using Microsoft Excel and PowerPoint, respectively. One upside of my years of service in this field remains an ability to make a spreadsheet do just about anything. At my peak, I could probably have built Facebook out of Excel. I was *that* good.

I spent roughly eight years, full-time and as a contractor, in this field, flying around the country, analyzing on this, strategizing on that, presenting in boardrooms, and participating in far too many conference calls. I've had desks arranged in an open-air bullpen. I've had cubicles. I've had offices with doors and *windows*. What I rarely had during these years was more than one or two other black people with whom to share the experience. And while I had experienced playing the role of black guy in a number of settings by this point in my life, Corporate America has a flavor all its own. For those of you who've done a tour of duty as a black person in Corporate America, I salute you. This chapter is written for you and all the brave souls who've served. For those who've served *with* them, this chapter is also for you. It's time for you to learn what it means to be The Black Employee.

SO YOU GOT A job in an office, you're one of the few minorities and possibly the only black person. First of all, congratulations on having obtained a job. In this economy, that is amazing and makes you a superhero. Protect the job at all costs! Second, I'm so sorry for the awkwardness you have endured or will endure in this environment. Hopefully this guide will help you weather the scenarios ahead or give you a different perspective on those you've already managed.

In many ways this guide is related to the chapter on "How to Be The Black Friend," with the difference being, your coworkers are not your friends. It's also closely connected to "How to Speak for All Black People," so please review both of these chapters to adequately prepare for your role as The Black Employee.

The truth is, you have two jobs.

The first is the explicit job for which you were hired. This is the job you saw posted on the Web or heard about through a friend. It's the job title printed on your business card and in the company directory. It's what you put on your LinkedIn profile.

For the sake of argument, let's say the job was research associate at Optimus Research Group.* When you heard about this posi-

---

* At the time of this writing, I could find no business named Optimus Research Group. In the event that such a company is formed by the time you read this, I sincerely apologize for unintentionally besmirching that organization's reputation in the name of this teachable moment. Any similarities between this thought exercise—this includes names, company activities, job positions, and the number of minority employees—and the actual work environment at Optimus Research

tion, you were excited. Why? Because you love research, and you're good at it. You prepared yourself. You updated your résumé. You boosted your past research experience and added personal details that connect you to the type of research this job requires. You read the company's website thoroughly. You Googled the business and its customers. You may even have done your own research on particular employees, especially management. You are prepared to be an excellent research associate, and when you get the job, and sign the papers, and show up for your first day, that's a role you are excited to play.

The thing is, you were also hired for another job: your blackness. That's not to say you were merely accepted due to some affirmative action quota. If that were the case, nothing more would be expected of you than simply being black and doing Job #1 above. That would make you a research associate who happens to be black. No, you have another job with specific responsibilities far beyond inhabiting your skin. The people who hired you likely weren't even conscious of this extra job. It's not as if they had one meeting about your research skills and another about your blackness talents. Nevertheless, they expect great things from you, even if subconsciously. In Job #2, you will be expected to:

- Part A: Represent the black community.
- Part B: Defend the company against charges of racism or lack of diversity.

Group are purely coincidental. Also, if Optimus does have a job opening for research associate, hook a brother up!

- Part C: Increase the coolness of the office environment by enthusiastically participating in company events.

If you interpret this job description a certain way, you might conclude that you have two, three, or even four jobs, because your blackness duty combines the roles of politician, lawyer, and entertainer. Now you're Jamaican! For the sake of simplicity and sanity, however, we will keep these jobs consolidated under the umbrella of Job #2.

Also of note, it is not a requirement that you fully embrace all parts of the second job. I'm merely informing you of the expectations. It's up to you to decide how good of a Black Employee you really want to be.

During your first days on the job, before diving into Parts A, B, and C of Job #2, there's something urgent you must do: *Spot the Negro.*

Like vampires and extremely rich people, black folk can sense one another. Use your Spidey Sense (Blacky Sense?*). Use your blackdar to inspect the workplace for signs of Other Negroes. They may be working security for the building. They may be in administrative support. They may be among the associate pool, or they may even be in upper management. Black folk can be anywhere. After all, *you're* here. But one of the biggest mistakes you can make as The Black Employee is to assume you are the only one. You were hired as a research associate, remember? So do some research!

If you find that there is another Black Employee, do not panic.

---

* No, don't call it a Blacky Sense. I regret typing that.

Employ the CARS system, as in *Collect* information, *Analyze* the data, *Review* your options, and *Set* your strategy. Like dogs sniffing each other's butts, you will need to figure out what your relationship to this other black person will be. How black do you expect him or her to be and vice versa? Is this the type of person who feels threatened by your presence? Does this person even acknowledge that he or she is black? You must find answers to all of these questions. Your career may depend on it. For example, if you sit in the middle of the corporate ladder and the other black person is a blue-collar employee, the last thing you want to do is alienate this person. He or she probably knows lots of office secrets, has read discarded memos, and can either make your life easier or make sure your office always smells like rotten fish. On the other hand, if The Other Negro is above you and older, she may see you as a small version of herself and offer mentorship, advanced warning on promotions, or just good information about what to avoid in the cafeteria. These and all other black-on-black intra-office interactions can be plotted on the Inter-Negro Spectrum of Hostility.* Whether you gain or lose in these relationships depends heavily on where the other black employee falls on the INSH.

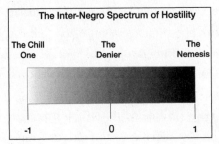

---

* The INSH is a proprietary scale developed by scholars at the Blackness Advanced Research Projects Agency (BARPA).

On one end, you have **The Chill One.**

This other black employee takes everything in stride. She acknowledges you in subtle ways, occasionally offers advice, and is overall an easygoing presence in the office and in your professional life. At a company meeting, when there's a mildly embarrassing racial moment, the two of you subtly smile at each other, connect eyes briefly, knowingly, and then return to business. Sometimes The Chill One will display light hints of subversion, but it's nothing over-the-top. For example, when the two of you are in the coffee room, she might say to you, "Hey, we should just take all these white people's shit and burn it." But then she laughs, and you laugh, and another coworker enters the room, asking, "What's so funny?" and without missing a beat you both say, "Tina Fey!"

My advice: if you encounter someone on the Chill end of the spectrum, be natural. This is the best type of other black employee to have.

At the other extreme of the Inter-Negro Spectrum of Hostility, you have **The Nemesis.**

This other black employee feels threatened by you. Everything is a competition. If you sign up for the community service committee, he brags about how much they got done last year. If you stay an hour late, he stays ninety minutes. He probably brandishes his education more than necessary, and he laughs too loud. He is naturally insecure, and your presence there serves to elevate his self-doubt further.

Do not respond directly to the competitive energy from The Nemesis. The best defense in this case is simply to do your job. You will probably find many opportunities to publicly undermine him, but don't. That's cruel. He's probably just scared because he's never not been the only black person before, and he's afraid you'll take his place. Take the high road. Be inclusive. Hopefully, with time, he will learn that there is room enough for two, maybe even three black people at this company.

At the very center of the spectrum you may encounter a type of black employee known as **The Denier**. This person simply does not acknowledge her race at all, perhaps hoping that by ignoring it, she'll never have to deal with any negativity associated with her race. While not explicitly combative with you, she's also unlikely to be a useful ally, especially if she ranks above you. It's not that she feels threatened by you. It's that she feels nothing. So she won't act to improve the situation at the company, either. Your best bet here is to accrue as much power in the company as you can so you can use your position for good and undo some of the damage caused by The Denier's apathy.

There's no guarantee you will be the only black employee, so I hope these descriptions help you orient yourself accordingly. Now, let's get into the details of your second job's requirements.

WHAT DO YOU THINK?

Your biggest Job #2 responsibility is to represent the black community (Part A). We addressed this function partially in the chapters "How to Speak for All Black People" and "How to Be The Black Friend." Representing the race spans many roles, but representing all of blackness as The Black Employee is unique. When you're vying for the spokesperson role on cable news, that's a conscious act and desire. You know what you're signing up for. When you entertain the questions and assumptions of your white friends, you have the mutual love and respect of your relationship with them to keep you motivated and temper your frustration. As The Black Employee, though, the potential upside is far more limited. There's no media exposure. There's no friendship. You just get irritated. You didn't sign up for this. You don't want to do this. You think, understandably, that *this is not your job*. My goal here is to gently remind you that *yes, this is your other job*.

So when you're in the elevator and a coworker asks, "Hey, Tiffany, Jim and I were wondering, are you disappointed with Obama?" you have some choices to make. The Black Friend would be honest and might go back and forth with your coworker on the substance of the question, relishing the opportunity to learn and enlighten. The Black Spokesperson would check his teeth for leftover food, adjust his blazer, and present a nuanced theory on the effectiveness of President Obama versus early expectations of his term, then attempt to get on MSNBC that night to say the same thing.

What you need to realize before opening your mouth is that although this appears to be a question for you to answer, it is, in fact, a setup for your coworkers to share their own ideas on the subject and passively seek validation of their opinions from you.

In this situation, The Black Employee has three basic options:

1. **Avoidance:** "You know, that's a really interesting question. I haven't spent much time thinking about it, honestly. These quarterly reports have been kicking my ass!"
2. **Confrontation:** "What? Are you asking me because I'm black?? You know we don't all think alike, right?"
3. **Answer the question:** "Honestly, I am a bit disappointed with President Obama. I'd still vote for him, but I feel

let down in a number of ways and think he hasn't been a strong enough advocate for working people."

Which option did you choose?

Let's review the possibilities.

Option 1 (avoidance) is a passive and polite way of telling someone to fuck off. You preserve a cordial and professional work environment and also manage to avoid getting any deeper into the subject. By pivoting the conversation back to work matters, you've effectively dodged the bullet. If you chose Option 1, you did well. This is an acceptable choice. If you're feeling generous that day, you could use the same deflective response but then add, "What do *you* think?" This will give your white colleagues the opening to express themselves they were hoping for. Whether you choose to listen to what he or she has to say is completely discretionary.

Option 2 (confrontation) is a risky move because it puts your coworkers on the defensive, and no one wants to be in that place. You're one step short of calling someone a racist, which is a far worse crime than actual racism. However, it's also a guaranteed method of drawing a clear boundary, and it discourages any similar inquiries in the future. If you choose the path of confrontation and rejection, you won't be the most liked employee, but being left alone leaves you time to focus on Job #1. Remember, you love research. If you chose Option 2, you did well. People will be less likely to engage you in office small talk of any kind, but that's likely a benefit when you consider the fact that every ten minutes of office small talk takes one year off of your life. If you are overly concerned about your coworkers' feelings, Option 2 is still available to you. Just make sure you deliver your response with a smile, maybe even a little laugh. Folks love happy black people, even when those black people are dissing them.

Option 3 (honesty) is a classic mistake. If you chose this, you have failed the exercise. Read carefully to understand why. You probably thought that by being honest, you were giving your coworker the benefit of the doubt. You're a good person, and that's a lovely way to live, on occasion, but under no circumstances should you tell your white coworkers what you actually think about a race-related matter! This leads to them sharing their own ideas, which leads to you getting upset, which leads to them wanting to talk about it even more, which leads to you getting even more upset. It's a vicious cycle, which likely ends in you storming out in the middle of a conference call, singing the Black National Anthem at the top of your lungs, and boarding the next flight to South Africa.

Even if your honesty in this case doesn't lead you to start roommate-hunting on Craigslist Johannesburg, answering the question with your true thoughts sends a signal to your white coworkers that you're down to play this game. Before long, you'll be on the receiving end of every black-related thought in the office, no matter how tenuous the connection:

"So, I was thinking of checking out this Ethiopian restaurant on Saturday. Have you heard anything about it?"

"I think it's so tragic the way the kids at that pool were discriminated against. Can you believe some people still think that way? I mean, it's the twenty-first century!"

"How do you get your hair to do that?? It's so cute! Can I touch it?"

By being too accommodating in some aspects of the implicit Job #2, you leave no time to do the explicit Job #1 and risk your position at the company. It's much less costly to avoid saying anything that commits you to a position (Option 1) or risk mildly hurting people's feelings but protecting your sanity (Option 2).

THE DIVERSITY COMMITTEE

Many U.S. companies understand the value of having a diverse workplace. They rightly believe that a variety of voices helping to shape their goods and services makes the entire enterprise more accessible to the increasingly diverse American consumer market. In order to demonstrate their commitment to this noble end, these companies create committees, diversity committees. Part A of Job #2 was all about your representing your people. By hiring you, the company really got all black people! Part B is about defending the company against charges of racism or lack of diversity, and your membership on the company's diversity committee is essential to fulfilling this job requirement.

The primary functions of the diversity committee are to establish meetings, generate reports, and use the word "diversity." A sample description might look like this:

> *Here at Optimus Research Group, we believe in three things: maximizing shareholder value, providing an exciting environment for professional development, and diversity. We heart diversity. Diversity is a core value and has been*

since our founding. The diversity committee embraces a diverse definition of diversity and seeks to provide programs and other opportunities that encourage knowledge of and respect for diversity. This includes, but is not limited to, race, gender, religion, age, sexual orientation, ethnicity, geography, socioeconomic background, taste in music, hairstyles, language, preferred airline, mental health status, body size, and mobile phone service provider.

The world is an increasingly diverse place, and to remain competitive, we must actively embrace a diverse mind-set in order to best tackle the diverse challenges ahead. With a diverse approach to diversity management, Optimus Research Group is positioned not just to survive in the changing marketplace but to thrive, becoming industry thought leaders on diversity.

As such, the diversity committee is responsible for leading efforts to proactively spread the values of diversity throughout the organization and meets monthly to ensure such projects are on track. The diversity committee will also create a task force to respond to any diversity issues raised by members of the diversity committee or other employees. The committee reports to the board of directors annually.

Remember, diversity is not a destination. It's a journey! So let's get on board!

Members of the Diversity Committee

The diversity committee is made up of a diverse set of people representing the strength of Optimus Research Group's commitment to diversity. The committee consists of five committed individuals.

Chair: Bob Bobson, CEO

Bob, who goes by "Bob" around the office, is the company CEO. He has always valued diversity and is known throughout the office for the diversity of ties he wears to work! His presence on the diversity committee is a symbolic and substantive testament to Optimus Research Group's commitment to diversity. Bob has two black friends and once ate a spicy meal at an Indian restaurant.

Vice Chair for Committee Diversity: Jennifer Claymore, HR Director

As the diversity committee's vice chair for diversity, Jen's role is to ensure diversity on the diversity committee. She assesses the committee's diversity on a quarterly basis using a diverse set of criteria. Jen loves world music.

Vice Chair for Diversity Outreach: Elaine Chu, Diversity Officer

Elaine joined Optimus Research Group because she has a passion for research matched only by her passion for diversity. With a Doctorate in Diversity Arts from Diversity University, Elaine brings a sophisticated and forward-thinking perspective on diversity matters. Elaine Chu is Asian.

Vice Chair for Diversity Task Force Creation: Doug Robinson, Senior Associate

Doug is responsible for the formation and organization of the committee's task forces in a manner consistent with the company's core value of diversity. Task forces Doug is most proud of include the Cinco de Mayo Task Force, the Remembering the Dream Task Force, and the Task Force Realignment Task Force. Doug is a big fan of The Wire.

Vice Chair for Applied Diversity: [Your Name Here], Research Associate

If your company does not have a diversity committee, congratulations, *you* are the diversity committee! Beyond your diversity committee membership, you must be active in at least two additional company activities to meet your Job #2 responsibility to protect the company against charges of racism:

THE COMPANY PHOTO

You will be very visible in the company photo, also the website and any other marketing materials. There's no way to avoid it. The photo will only be scheduled when you are in the office, so don't try pretending to be sick. They'll wait for you. And certainly don't think about hiding out in the background. Your face has to be clearly visible. There's even a chance you will be captured in these images if you don't work for the company. You might have gotten off the elevator at the wrong floor and wandered around only to discover later that you are the face of Optimus Research Group. Check the website to be sure this is not the case.

RECRUITING

You are going to the career fair. All career fairs. This is non-negotiable. You exist as physical proof to prospective employees that the company is actually diverse, and you will have to interact with job-seekers so they can see that you are real and not simply an advanced animatronic mannequin. But, if you come across a smart-mouthed kid who insists he's not interested because Optimus does work for the Defense Department, and "he doesn't want to kill people," don't bother trying to convince him otherwise.

Even bringing over a higher-ranking white colleague won't do the trick. Just move on.

OFFICE SOCIALIZING

You've repped your race. You've made the company look diverse. You're not finished with Job #2 yet. Fulfilling Part C (increase the coolness of the office environment by enthusiastically participating in company events) may prove to be the most emotionally and physically exhausting. Many people in The Black Employee role like to pretend there is no Part C and attempt to live two completely separate lives. This may describe you. You figure you can be one person at the office during the day and return to a more comfortable environment where you can be a different person at night, shunning all opportunities to socialize with your coworkers. Certainly it is understandable, especially if you are actively engaged in Blackness Parts A and B, that you would feel that you've done enough. You haven't.

Daytime activities

This is relatively easy. There will be office birthday parties, celebrations of promotions, and modest gatherings to cheer the achievement of big business milestones. Your job is just to be there. For extra points, smile and look like you're enjoying yourself. Maybe even crack a joke! Your comfort is in the back of nearly everyone's mind, so if you can put them at ease by acting like you really want to be there, you'll be doing an excellent job of being The Black Employee.

After-hours socializing

Depending on your own background and life experiences, this may or may not be new to you, but after an eight-to-twelve-hour day, white office workers often don't feel like they've spent enough time with each other. Therefore, they are prone to organizing pseudo-official company activities such as bowling or happy hour. If you are invited, you should make the occasional effort to go. Continually declining this invitation will slowly lead to your being cut off from all advancement opportunities. Whereas, if you say yes, you will make your coworkers so happy! You will also get valuable inside dirt on company politics, business affairs, and general gossip. It may feel petty, but your prospects in Job #1 (remember, that research associate position you love so much?) can be heavily influenced by your performance in Job #2, often in subtle ways. What I'm saying is, go out drinking with your coworkers from time to time. Your job doesn't stop when you leave the building.

The company holiday party

This is not as simple as the prior activities. In fact, I want you to pause right now. Take a deep breath. Stand up. Stretch a little. Maybe walk around the room you're in and focus your eyes on something in the distance before resuming this lesson. The company holiday party is no joke, and much will be expected of you. If you don't bring your A-game, all that you've gained from faithful execution of the advice mentioned could be placed in serious jeopardy.

A company holiday party is a perfect storm of factors that include the presence of:

- Non-employees, including spouses, significant others, and dates
- Food and beverage, especially alcohol
- Possible music and dancing

Each of these provides an opportunity for you to fly or fumble, so you must approach the night with your eyes wide-open.

Your date

The first thing you must consider is whom to bring with you. You know your coworkers better than your prospective date. How will your date interact with them? Will he or she fit in, get by, or actually cause some sort of ruckus? Does he or she work in a similar environment and thus have the experience and wisdom to deal with what nightmares may come? It's better to attend alone than bring someone wholly unprepared, who might, for example, mouth off to your boss about how you "really" feel about the company or let slip your plans to leave for another company. That said, having an ally present who fully understands you can be a great asset, so my advice is bring someone if you have someone to bring, but give this person a comprehensive briefing before you throw him or her into a potential combat situation.

Your food

Often these events are catered, and if you're in the job long enough you will face a food choice dreaded by black people since breaking the Corporate America color line: whether or not to eat the watermelon. First of all, don't panic. I know what it's like. You're not alone. Many more like you have survived this situation, so have faith in yourself and your people. Now, take a closer look. Is it the only fruit? Is it arranged on its own plate adjacent to other segregated fruits? Is it mixed in with a fruit salad? Again, take a brief moment. Smile at the person across from you in the buffet line. We're going to get through this together.

The most important thing in this situation is not to draw attention to yourself. Don't deliberate too long. It is worse to make no choice than to linger too long on what choice to make. If people notice you thinking about it, they'll put two and two together. They'll assume you're stuck because you can't decide if you should just devour all available watermelon right there from the line. So, yes, remain calm, but also just do *something*. If watermelon is the only fruit, you are in the clear, and the gods are with you. No one can read into your choice if you never really had a choice. Enjoy it, and congratulations! Watermelon is delicious.

If there are segregated plates of fruit, I suggest a four-to-one ratio of non-watermelon to watermelon. Look, they know you want it. *You* know you want it. So if you conspicuously avoid it, that's an admission right there: guilt by omission. In the case of a mixed-fruit bowl, you will have to be comfortable with the unknown. In this case, leave it to fate. If you dip that oversize spoon into the bowl, and it comes back full of nothing but watermelon, so be it. Start singing the theme song to *Good Times*, and just roll with the absurdity of the moment. In this unlikely event, I recommend you joke about it with other employees, because if you don't, they'll assume you have some magical powers of watermelon magnetism, and that's not an idea we want out in the world.[*]

Your drinking

There may be a relatively open bar situation at this party. Even more than the watermelon threat, in this arena, you Must. Be. Extremely. Careful. Unlike after-work drinks with colleagues, the company holiday party lasts longer, and people get looser. Also, everyone will be there. Marriages have ended because someone drank too much and said the wrong thing or grabbed the wrong part of the wrong person at the company holiday party. You cannot afford this. You are a rare representative of your kind. Think about your people!

While everyone around you may decide to let it all hang out, you have a responsibility to maintain a bit more control. Don't drink too much. Don't end up alone with someone else's date. And when anyone at all asks you how you like working at the company, you tell that person you fucking love it here and can't imagine working with a better group of people.

Your dancing

If there's music and at least a four-square-foot area of floor, people are going to dance, and they are going to expect you to join them. That's the way it is. Most Americans have grown up on a steady media diet of well-choreographed dancing by black people. You have big, custom-made, Hollywood-backed shoes to fill.

---

[*] We have managed to keep this power secret for centuries. Don't blow it all because you couldn't create an effective distraction.

If you are not a good dancer, that's fine. It really is. Just make sure to compensate by keeping a drink in your hand and being extra-talkative. Not every black person can dance or enjoys the act. President Obama can't dance. We all saw him on *The Ellen DeGeneres Show*, and we got over it. Your coworkers will get over it, too.

The greater peril exists for those who actually *can* dance.* Proceed with extreme caution.

If you are a good dancer and actually enjoy it, you should ease into the act. Hang out on the edge of the dance floor and two-step to the beat. Then walk away. A few songs later, come back and do the same, maybe adding a little something extra but always making sure to include your coworkers in your moves. For some of you this will be difficult, because you're so naturally good, and dancing brings such joy, but you must fight the instinct to go rogue and launch into a Soul Train Moment.†

Once you go down the path of the Soul Train Moment, there is no return. Your coworkers are biologically programmed to form a circle around you, start clapping and chanting your name. At first, you think, "This is great! I'm amazing! I'm the best dancer in the world!" After three songs, however, you start to feel a little tired and a bit thirsty. You slow down, and start looking for a

---

* For the record, I'm a very good dancer. I'm generally the best dancer on whatever side of the Mississippi River I'm on. True story.

† A Soul Train Moment is when you just get hit with the beat, forget where you are, and start going all out like you were with your friends. You start busting moves, spinning, and displaying complex bodily rhythm and coordination. You do what the saying says and actually "dance like nobody's watching," forgetting that *everybody is watching.*

crack in the circle so you can return to your table and grab some water. You realize you can't see your date. You just want to go, but you can't. Because now you've excited the mob, and they keep chanting, "Go [Your Name]! Go [Your Name]!" and they make sure the DJ keeps it on hip-hop 'cause that's what you like, and when you try to push your way out of the circle, your cubicle mate exclaims, "Whoa! I had no idea you were such a great dancer! You're like the best dancer ever!" and then he pretends to keep up with you for a while, puts his arm around your shoulders, and whispers in your ear, "If you ever want to see your date again, you'll keep dancing."

Now you're scared, so you dance harder, and you give in to the moment, and you think, "This can't get any worse and eventually these people will get tired, and I'll rescue my date, and we'll leave." But before that can happen, something worse happens. There's *another* black person at the party. You don't know who he is or where he came from. He could be somebody's boyfriend. He could be the bartender. He could be some brother off the street that your coworkers paid to come in at this very moment. *None of this matters.* What matters is that he has found his way into your dance circle, and he's *challenging* you!

Instinct takes over, and you square off. Pretty soon the two of you are engaged in an epic dance battle. You're literally putting on a show at this point, and it covers the entire history of modern black dance. You jump between Lindy Hop, Cabbage Patch, Running Man, Samba, the Harlem Shuffle, the Robot, Beyoncé's *Single Ladies* dance, the Percolator, the Diddy Bop (which you hate!), the Moonwalk, Some New Thing You Two Just Made Up, and you're actually teaching people how to Dougie! You are determined to defeat this Random Brother and prove that "These are *my* white people!"*

Eventually, Random Brother stands down. Meanwhile, your white people hoist you up on their shoulders, outdoing each other with praise for your astounding talent, satisfied that they know the Best Black Person Ever. You find your date and head home, exhausted and relieved that the ordeal is over.

But it isn't. Because now they know your secret, and they can never ever let you rest. You are destined to top your dance performance at every company holiday party for as long as you work at this company.

Congratulations, and I'm sorry. You are The Black Employee.

---

* I would like to thank comedian Reese Waters for teaching me this expression in a joke of his about dancing with white people. He also gave me permission to use it in this book, so you should Google him and go to all of his shows to the point where you start to make him feel uncomfortable. Also, ask him to dance.

How to Be The Angry Negro

I 'M A *really* nice guy. I like to smile. I have a naturally diplomatic disposition, and I'd generally rather reason with you and use humor than argue or fight. But there are times when my mother's take-no-bullshit attitude emerges, and I invite confrontation and put my anger as a black person on full display. In high school, when I worked as an aide at the *Washington Post*, I would wear provocative T-shirts with messages like DANGER! EDUCATED BLACK MAN. I *wanted* people to ask me, "What's so dangerous about an educated black man?" just so I could respond, "Because he'll realize how unjust this country is and want to change it!" at which point the questioner would flee, or so I fantasized. When my school principal openly supported what I considered to be racially driven and unjust decision to cancel the Black Student Union dance, I had a one-on-one meeting with him, lost my cool, stormed out of the room, slammed the door, and screamed, "This school is so racist!" Then I ran some laps to try to chill out. So many of my experiences have been about the transition into the mainstream and how to balance blackness within a larger context, but this isn't always possible. Given how much we've shared together so far, I think you're ready to meet The Angry Negro.

SOMETIMES IN AMERICA BEING black demands that one get angry. Much of that rage is anchored in history. There are obvious factors at play: slavery, for example. The treatment of black folks as property seems to have had an effect on our position and prospects here. The subsequent state-sponsored or -supported discrimination and terrorism—I'm thinking environmental racism, police brutality, lynchings, separate and unequal schooling, neighborhood redlining, et cetera—have also cast a long shadow over the current black experience in the United States.

One in fifteen black male adults is behind bars (compared to one in a hundred U.S. adults overall);[*] black household wealth averages just one-twentieth that of whites,[†] having fallen precipitously after the housing crisis; black people in Texas have a habit of finding themselves under the wheels of trucks driven by racists; and then there's BET. There is no shortage of issues for which a black person in America can justifiably get mad. The Angry Negro is the personification of that Black Rage.

---

[*] According to the 2008 Pew Center on the States report "One in 100: Behind Bars in America 2008."

[†] According to the 2011 Pew Research Center report "Wealth Gaps Rise to Record Highs Between Whites, Blacks, Hispanics."

As The Angry Negro, you are committing yourself to a life of hate. You are agreeing to be always disagreeable. You are shameless. You are unforgiving. You only see the world through race-tinted glasses. You are, basically, an asshole. That's what embodying the collective ills of a people can do to you.

You don't make excuses for offhand, offensive comments.

You don't seek to understand "the other side." You see everything in terms of our side versus the side that enslaved, ridiculed, wrongfully imprisoned, and impoverished your people. You already know everything you need to know about how the other side thinks. You wear the scars of its philosophy.

You are compelled to say what others won't. They remain quiet, not because they doubt the truth of their perceptions but because they lack the courage to risk being ostracized and being labeled "The Angry Negro." You have no such hesitation. You relish being so labeled. Rage is your cape. Self-confidence is your mask. Truth is your sword.

If the above sounds appealing to you or just sounds like something you'd like to try out for a while, check out the excerpt below from the *Operating Manual for The Angry Negro Persona*.

Preface your answer to all questions with "as a black man" or "as a black woman," depending on your gender.

Q: Do you approve of the job President Obama is doing?

A: As a black woman, I resent the assumption you've made that I have an opinion on the matter. What, just because I'm black, I need to have some kind of position on the black president? How did you feel about that last white *president? I'm tired of being profiled like this. You are violating my civil rights, and I will not stand for it! My people did not build this country just so you could ask me about the black president!*

Q: *Did you see the news report last night about that apartment fire?*

A: *As a black man, I understand all too well the struggles of the dispossessed and the conflagration of injustice leading to such a state. This world is a farce.*

Q: *Would you like paper or plastic?*

A: *As a black woman, I choose paper. Its brownness reminds me of my people. The tree that died so it might hold these heavy groceries is a metaphor for the sufferance of my people, who, for too long, have carried the burden of America's original sin. Its roots run as deep as the blood of my people beneath this so-called nation. [Liberal usage of "so-called" is highly encouraged.]*

MAXIMIZE THE DISCOMFORT OF WHITE PEOPLE

White people's comfort is not your concern. In fact, when around white people, you take great pleasure in making them feel uncomfortable. This doesn't have to depend on them prompting you with some race-related question. It's actually better if the subject of race is nowhere near the conversation.

For example, when in an elevator with one or more white people, quietly but firmly say something like the following:

"It wasn't that long ago that people like me weren't allowed in this elevator. The good old days, huh?"

Don't address your question directly to the white person. It's more uncomfortable if you just let it hang in the air while looking in no particular direction. The age and location of the elevator are not important. You just want these white people to know that you know that their days of openly discriminating against black people are over, not that these particular white people ever did that.

Another tactic you might try is to directly confront white people over how open-minded they are. It is perfectly acceptable to do this for white people you know well or barely at all.

Perhaps White Jim is talking about a new bicycle he just got or his favorite television program. Your job is to throw a racial wrench into the operation with a question like, "Jim, I was just curious. How many black friends do you actually have?" This will have the immediate effect of throwing off Jim's equilibrium and forcing him into a defensive state of mind. He's sure he didn't do anything wrong, but he can't help feeling as if he must prove that point.

If Jim has an answer, you attack: "Three? You actually keep count of all your black friends? Really, Jim?"

If Jim says he has none, you also attack: "So you mean to tell me you haven't found even one black person worthy of your friendship? Man, that's just sad."

Regardless of what Jim says, you attack. That's the point. Attack White Jim.

MAXIMIZE THE DISCOMFORT OF BLACK PEOPLE

Do not expend your rage solely on white people. Think bigger. From your point of view, your black friends and associates and even black strangers cannot be black enough. It's not always their fault, but you do get tired of being the consciousness of the group. They've been so brainwashed by mainstream society, so mis-educated, that you understand it's up to you to set them on a more correct course, especially if they seem to reject your solutions.

Many of the black people around you act like race doesn't define everything in the world. It's your job to remind them that it does!

Let's say one of your black friends is having a problem with her boss. To you, it's obvious that this is an example of The White Man holding a sister back. Your friend may try to explain to you that her boss isn't white and that the problem stems from her poor performance on a previous assignment, but you're not having any excuses like that. In America, a black woman just can't catch a break, and you remind her of this at a very high volume by saying, "In America! A black woman just can't catch a break!"

When communicating with your fellow black people, make sure to sprinkle your speech with a lot of "my brotha!" and "my sistah!" language. This adds credibility to your case and builds a connection with any other black person around you at the time.

So, when you see a black man reading the *New York Times* . . .

"My brotha! I see you are filling your mind with The White Man's lies again. The mis-education of the Negro continues!"

The same style can be used in any situation. The point is simply to remind these Negroes that they are black!

"You actually support a football team named the 'Washington Redskins?' My brotha, how can you be so ignorant?"

"Skiing, my sistah? Are you so obsessed with whiteness that you must frolic in it?"

"So, we're eating Cheetos now, are we, my brotha?"

And so forth . . .

Your job, although it may at times appear to be purely symbolic and over-the-top, has real value. You will confront politicians, police officers, business owners, anyone. You are fearless. You're an angry black superhero for justice. Remember that when people inevitably start to distance themselves from you. Being hated is part of the job.

How to Be The (Next) Black President

*We need a new black leader. That's why I hope the black
leader we get is Barack Obama, the black senator from
Illinois. That dude is cool. People say he's going to be president
someday. My question is, president of what? 'Cause one day
there may be a black president, but there will never be a black
president named Barack Obama! Ladies and gentlemen,
that's too black. That dude's name might as well be Blacky
Blackerson.*

— W. Kamau Bell, on Comedy Central in 2005*

YOU DIDN'T think I could write a book called *How to Be Black*
and not talk about the black president, did you? Come on, y'all!

Getting the job of first black president was hard. Keeping it
is harder. Prior to Barack Obama the only way Americans could
experience a black president was through television and film.

---

* Comedy Central refers to this as "the first Barack Obama joke."

The most recent black TV presidents all had amazing flaws or challenges. On *24*, President David Palmer (played by Dennis Haysbert) was assassinated after three failed attempts on his life. When his brother was elected, he was immediately targeted for assassination as well! In *Idiocracy*, President Camacho is a former wrestler and porn star. Need I say more? *The Fifth Element*'s President Lindberg was probably the coolest black president on screen, and he presided over the entire galaxy, but I had a hard time not seeing actor Tom Lister Jr. as his more famous, decidedly non-presidential character Deebo from *Friday*. Maybe it's my own fault but I kept expecting the galactic president to go around stealing people's bikes and weed. Beyond these on-screen moments, the only other pre-Obama black president America experienced was the regrettable literary flourish of Toni Morrison, who dubbed Bill Clinton our "first black president."*

When Obama came along, I campaigned so intensely for him I felt like *I* was running for president. My friends jokingly referred to me as "Barackatunde." When he won the Iowa Caucuses, I screamed, "*We* won!" I hit the road hard in Northern Virginia, Philadelphia, and South Dallas, canvassing, phone-banking, and occasionally speechifying. I personally experienced many of the frustrating racial ups and downs and hopes and fears of the campaign. In South Dallas, where I helped fix a voting machine no one had seen before, the elderly black election official exclaimed, "I think God sent you here to save this election." On CNN just after Iowa, I shared a segment with Reverend Jesse Jackson and

---

* *The New Yorker.* October 1998. Never forget.

found myself in the odd position of trying to lift the mood after he exclusively focused on all the things that could go wrong.

Online at *Jack & Jill Politics*, the blog I cofounded with Cheryl Contee, we were like a messaging army, especially when it came to the treatment of this black presidential candidate by the media, the opposition, and even traditional black leadership.

In the beginning, Obama wasn't black enough for some. Many white journalists excitedly pointed out how atypical Obama was with his biraciality, advanced degrees, and articulateness. But the idea that Obama wasn't *that* black went far beyond out-of-touch media and infected out-of-touch (or jealous) older black leaders. Civil rights leader and former U.S. ambassador Andrew Young answered questions no one was asking when he claimed, "Bill [Clinton] is every bit as black as Barack. He's probably gone with more black women than Barack." Ha ha.

As Obama's victories piled up, he was too black for others. His relationship with Reverend Wright dominated media coverage for months, with folks painting this Harvard Law School graduate as some sort of radical black revolutionary. The man felt so pressured that he gave a special address just about race! Today, you can find more Obama-as-super-threatening-black-guy coverage in just about any report from Fox News. "Black president wants to kill your grandma!" "Black president wants to take your money!" "Black president wants to let the Mexicans eat your children. *With salsa!*" "Black president flew planes into the World Trade Center!"

Yet others took a measured but still optimistic tone in their endorsements. I recall such a moment at the Apollo Theater in December 2007, when I saw the Princeton professor Cornel West enthusiastically endorse candidate Obama. One of his main points was the risk of expecting too much from this man. As I wrote then of the event:

> With his trademark uneven afro, thin black scarf,
> black three-piece suit, and verbal dexterity, West brought
> historical context to the evening, reminding us of the long
> history of black activists and artists whose words and deeds
> found a home at the Apollo. He spoke of Obama glowingly:
> "It's not because he's intelligent and articulate. I expect
> black folk from Harvard to be articulate. But Barack is
> also eloquent . . ."
>
> Most valuable to me was West's warning not to see in
> Barack something he is not: a reincarnation of some great
> black hope from days gone by: "We don't expect Alicia
> Keys to be Sarah Vaughn, and we should not expect Barack
> Obama to be Frederick Douglass. He is his momma's son
> and his daddy's son," and, West continued, he is who we
> need in this country today.

Yet now that Obama is in office, West, too, has had a change of heart, referring to President Obama in 2011 as a "black mascot of Wall Street oligarchs and a black puppet of corporate plutocrats." The man who embraced and praised candidate Obama's biracial identity in 2007 attempted to undermine the authenticity of his American blackness in 2011 by implying that Obama's white mother and lack of slave blood made him afraid of "free black men," and bitterly complained that Obama dissed him at inauguration and spent too much time in the company of Jews.

Contradictory expectations, perceptions, and criticisms come with the job for any president, but the special turmoil around race is a unique feature of a black U.S. presidency, and Obama's campaign and first term should serve as a valuable model for those of you who might pursue that path someday.

Unlike several of the other chapters in this book, this guide to the presidency is unlikely to be used in a practical sense by most of you. While we can all be employees and friends and spokespeople and angry, very few of us have any chance of becoming commander-in-chief. But just because something is unlikely does not mean we shouldn't prepare ourselves for the eventuality.

Most of us will not be in the room when someone is choking, but we have been trained in the Heimlich maneuver. Most of us will never find ourselves engulfed in flames, but we probably have memorized the "stop, drop, and roll" technique. And most of us will never know what it feels like to take the oath of office under the direction of the Chief Justice of the United States Supreme Court on a crisp January day, but that is no excuse to avoid the lessons of a black presidency.

What does the election of the First Black President mean for those who would be The *Second* Black President or *Third* or even, and this is crazy, The *Fourth* Black President?

Despite your having lost the race to break the presidential color line, the odds of a black presidency are higher post-Obama than they were pre-Obama. He has established a precedent. Yet slightly higher odds do not imply ease. Know this going in, and remember John F. Kennedy's words: "We do these things not because they are easy, but because they are hard."

The American presidency is one of the most important roles in the world. From this position, one can shift a nation's priorities, drive the news cycle, and eradicate large groups of brown people overseas with the signing of an executive order. Granted, CEOs of multinational companies also wield similar power, but there's still nothing quite like occupying the Office of the President. You get a plane, your own seal, and an honor guard! It could be you, and when you wake up handcuffed to a briefcase with the nuclear launch codes inside, you'll be glad you read this guide.

IDEAL CONDITIONS FOR YOU TO BECOME PRESIDENT

Let's start with your campaign. In order to become president, you'll need a bit of campaign luck. Every past president depended on a bit of luck to win the office, but you'll require heaps of it. Any of the following conditions will significantly boost your odds of moving into 1600 Pennsylvania Avenue.

1. An exceptionally mediocre sitting president

When you run, you want the sitting president to have high disapproval ratings even among members of his own party. The entire country should prefer to have the president tarred and feathered while strapped to a scooter careening downhill into molten lava than commit him to signing another piece of legislation into law.

Only in such an environment will people even notice you, and even then, there's no guarantee they'll take you seriously.*

---

* Just ask Texas congressman Ron Paul.

2. An uninspiring and dangerous general election opponent

It will be an extraordinary event if you are able to earn your party's nomination, but your real battle only just begins at this point. Your ideal general election opponent should be someone who feels exactly wrong for this particular moment in U.S. history. If the country needs new blood and energy, you want an opponent who is the physical embodiment of age and lethargy. Ideally, the public can better imagine your opponent telling a group of children to get off his or her lawn than they can picture this hypothetical president delivering an inspiring State of the Union address.

If the country needs a calm, steady hand, your ideal opponent is rash and explosive. If the country needs worldliness, your opponent will be proud to have never left her state or speak foreign languages.

You'll know you've got an actual shot if your opponent or your opponent's running mate feels plucked from the pages of a dystopian political satire. If your opponent's vice-presidential candidate frightens the public more than the top of the ticket, this is great for you.

3. The feeling that America is on the actual brink of collapse

The country should be in an extremely terrible state. It's not enough to have economic problems, wars, increasing international competition, and a global crisis. All those things may help you, but to get the maximum boost, you want a severe economic crisis the likes of which hasn't been experienced for several generations, and just when people think it's over you'll want another one and then another one right after that. You'll need multiple wars, none of which is going particularly well, but all of which are draining the nation's treasury. You'll be helped significantly by a general feeling in the country that it's not progressing nearly as fast as the rest of the world on any number of indicators, and some Americans seriously considering emigration to unthinkable destinations such as France, Costa Rica, or Libya.

And, the coup de grâce: your prospects will brighten if people actually fear the wholesale extinction of the human race, perhaps due to the recent discovery of an invading alien army or the catastrophic ignition of an Earth-destroying doomsday device by a megalomaniacal, evil super-villain. If people literally feel that they have *nothing* to lose, you could very well win!

4. Your ability to "look presidential"

Many smart, qualified people have run for president. Many smarter and more qualified people have never even tried. The difference between those who should be president and those who make it far in the process often comes down to who looks and feels like they could actually be the president.

For you it means your résumé has got to be top-notch. It will help tremendously if you've got a degree from an Ivy League university, but it will help even more if you have five. You'll go further if your family is attractive and has no known criminal record. I know some candidates with troubled family connections have made it far in the past, but the rules are more stringent for you.

Clearly, this is a lot to ask for, but I'm just laying out the *ideal* circumstances. There's no guarantee any of these conditions will come to pass, and only the direct intervention of God could explain if they all existed at the same time, but if you are fortunate enough to be able to run under at least one of these conditions, you'll have a real shot at becoming the next Barack Obama.

WHAT YOUR CANDIDACY MEANS

Politicians constantly make the mistake of thinking that their campaigns are about *them*. They are not. Political campaigns are about the people and what they need or want at a particular moment in space and time. The candidate lucky enough to channel the mood of the people and feel authentically connected to it has a higher chance of winning, so it's critical that you understand not what your candidacy means to you, but what it means to the people.

The mere fact that you are running will always shine brightly as a symbol of potential racial reconciliation in America. It is to your advantage that no one expects you to run. Many will assume that Obama's experience in the White House would be enough to dissuade any additional black contenders. In fact, part of his tough road may be designed to prevent *you* from running. America looks askance at black people who give back to the nation, because America knows she hasn't been historically kind to her citizens of African descent. Expect there to be some suspicion about your motives for running. Really, why would a black person want this responsibility, *again*? At the same time, because you're black and taking this on, you give significant numbers of people hope. You let them breathe a sigh of relief, if not about *all* black people, then certainly about you.

America dodged a bullet in the 1960s when cities burned in response to the Vietnam War, assassinations, and large-scale police brutality. Since then, there's always the concern that our nation's black population will rise up Nat Turner–style and exact revenge through violent revolution. Much of this rage has been effectively muted and channeled into commercial hip-hop, unrealistic dreams of professional sports careers, and daily doses of poison masquerading as nutrition in the form of poorly stocked grocery stores and fast-food businesses in black neighborhoods. There's just not a lot of rioting energy left, with so many distractions.

By running for president, you're demonstrating that you see politics, not violent revolution, as the appropriate arena for addressing these issues. You cause mainstream minds to pause and say, "Whoa, check it out. Black person's running for president again. Black person hasn't given up on her country. How 'bout that? We got another chance after all!"

Far more than a politician or candidate, you are a symbol, and symbols are powerful.

This worked really well for Obama and can probably be used one more time to great effect. You don't have to explicitly say you will heal the racial divide. The better you do in your campaign, the more people will assume you are the healer for whom we've been waiting. Here, a balancing act is required. On the one hand, avoid explicitly accepting the responsibility of Racial Healer. Obama made this mistake, holding inaugural events in the shadows of Dr. King, invoking the memories of the Civil Rights Movement, speaking all inspirationally and stuff. To appear to embrace the Racial Healer role openly would invite criticisms about your arrogance. On the other hand, do not go out of your way to deny it, either. Your electoral success depends on significant numbers of people projecting their intimate hopes and aspirations onto your campaign. Having an effective campaign message and strategy is great. Making millions of dreams come true is much better. The best marketing minds in corporate America have figured this out. Just let it happen.

The black problem

I'm not going to dance delicately around this. Do not mention black people.

If you truly and unavoidably feel you must, speak of them as a parent to a child requiring discipline. The freedom with which you're allowed to mention black people depends heavily on what you are saying. If you are criticizing black behavior or calling on black people to do more for themselves, you can spend all day and all night talking about black people. America loves to hear leaders demanding that folks do more to better themselves.

Just be sure to avoid implying that any collective effort is required to help one group of people improve their situation. Americans believe strongly in the myth of rugged individualism and self-made superstars. Don't undermine this belief by bringing up group grievances. (Of course, if you're a conservative candidate, your entire platform consists of this message.) You can't get by with telling folks, "God helps those who help themselves," alone. You've got to speak to various interest groups and convince them that you understand their problems and have their back.

With most groups, this will not pose any problems. You should feel free to highlight the challenges you see and solutions you have in mind for women, Latinos, Jews, Asians, farmers, students, small-business owners, Christians, artists, technologists, cobblers, medical practitioners, chimney sweeps, and Nate Walsh of Dayton, Ohio.

However, you cannot come right out and make promises to black voters in public. It's what white people expect and fear, so you have to be extremely careful in how you refer to your own people. Any time you're talking about issues that especially affect black Americans, try to couch it in a more universal light. For example, use the term "middle class." Very few people can criticize you for promising to help the middle class, because in America, everyone sees him- or herself as middle-class. Millionaires think they are middle-class. The three-years-unemployed real estate broker thinks of herself as middle-class as well. "Middle class" is the great normalizing phrase of our time. On the other hand, if you say "Black Americans," white people will know exactly whom you mean, and your cover will be blown.

Under special circumstances, you *can* refer to "urban communities," but for God's sake be careful. It is a cloaking device with very limited power. In the late 1990s, radio stations started changing their descriptions from "black" to "urban" programming, but nothing else changed, just the label. "Urban" has a softer sound than "black." "Urban" makes people feel like they are on a mildly risky but ultimately safe municipal safari. "Black" makes them lock their car doors. The more the term "urban" is used, though, the more people figure out what you're really saying.

Hire lots of white people on your campaign staff

You want a staff that is going to put America at ease and present you as a non-threat. The best way to do this is with lots and lots of white people, just hordes of them. Visitors to your campaign headquarters should find white people pouring out of every opened door or drawer, spilling onto the floor like bubbles from a malfunctioning washing machine. White people love to listen to other white people, and seeing large groups of enthusiastic black people is unnerving.

Don't be too self-confident

People love a leader with confidence, but as a black presidential candidate you have to walk a delicate line between calling attention to your talents and portraying the humble, reluctant public servant. Black people who think too much of themselves are a turn-off, so try to avoid coming across that way.

Expect haters from all sides

Keep a copy of your birth certificate on your body at all times, even in the shower. Use Ziploc bags and Velcro to make sure you never drop it. President Obama made the mistake of thinking that newspaper records, the word of the State of Hawaii, and common sense would eventually prevail over rumors that he was born during a celebration of the Fourth Intifada in the fiery pit of Mount Doom, somewhere in the Marxist Russian province of Kenya. You cannot afford such distractions. A permanently visible birth certificate hanging around your neck, open to inspection by any white American citizen at any time, should do the trick. To be safe, also run a high-definition video loop of your live birth in a special section of your campaign website. The video should contain a clear shot of that day's newspaper as well as a verifiably American city skyline in the background.

Meanwhile, be prepared for some black people to claim that you are not black enough, because of your appeal to large numbers of non-blacks. For these people, part of the very definition of blackness is being shut out of the corridors of power. Once a black person gets inside, he or she necessarily loses their all-access pass to the black community. I advise you to ignore these particular black people.

You might not win

You don't have to win to have an effect. It helps if you raise a decent amount of money and place well during the primaries, hold your own in the debates, and so forth. But you win a symbolic victory just by putting your hat in the ring. Feel good about this. You're basically a candidate for America's Black Friend (move over, Denzel!), and we all know what a racial-divide-healing and important role that is.

BUT IF YOU DO WIN . . .

Congratulations! You've made it. You followed the playbook above and improvised as the situation demanded, and now you are the top employee in the United States federal government. Let's get to work. Here's your assignment if you want to keep this shiny new job of yours.

Reach out to your worst enemies

As with the campaign, you cannot show favoritism to your race or even to your party. The best way to maintain this impression is to regularly talk up the value of your political opponents. Meet with them. Refer to their "good ideas" in your speeches. Make a big show of reaching across the aisle. Remember, if you fail to preside with enough humility, you will be seen as The Angry Negro, and you can't hold that job and this one at the same time.

Be cool

This shouldn't be too hard, because America generally thinks black people are cool. Just ride the wave, even if you can't dance.

Don't change too many things

Fortunately for you, the president isn't nearly as powerful as the public assumes, and the wheels of government turn slowly if they turn at all. Still, you want to be careful not to rush too many changes through. Try not to forget that *you* are the change, and a pretty big one at that. You are the *second black president*! The first black president could have been a fluke. There are always voting machine errors and irrational exuberance to explain that away. After Obama, a number of people in this country will be relieved and ready to return to "regular" presidents. A second black president means people know what they were doing. The second black president is actually the first black president! Just remember the lessons of Obama, and do not ask the country to accept you as president along with your campaign agenda. It's a big pill to swallow just to have a black president. Having a black president who actually does what he or she campaigned for is taking things a bit far. Don't be greedy.

Occasionally remind the country that you aren't really that black

You cannot overestimate the degree to which your presidency threatens millions of citizens. They are waiting for you to show that you're out for racial revenge, and avoiding black issues and direct eye contact with black people just is not enough to satisfy folks. Your avoidance of direct "black issues" during the campaign was a good start, but you're going to have to show the American people you mean business when you're president as well.

I'm not saying you can't actually do things. I'm saying you have to be very careful about how you do them. If you want to address educational outcomes, criminal justice, wealth disparity, teen pregnancy, that's all well and good, but when you give your big speeches (yes, you're going to have to give lots of big inspirational speeches, because Obama set the bar pretty high), you cannot come right out and say you want to address these issues. It's terrifying to the majority.

To limit that fear, every once in a while, you're going to have to sacrifice one of your own. This will show those most fearful of your power that you're not *that* black of a president. It's a test, just like the one Job faced when God allowed Satan to test his faith. A lot of innocent people died in the Book of Job, but he passed the test and got a book in the Bible named after him. Don't you want that?

At the first sign that the opposition is targeting a black member of your administration (and they will), you have to execute the person. Obama could get away with "distancing" himself from some and "letting go" of others. For you, the bar is higher. Of course you're busy, so you can't be responsible for all the staffing and un-staffing decisions, but just make sure there is a clear, zero-tolerance policy in your administration for defending black administration officials, and keep a firing squad or electric chair in some corner of the White House. Defending black government employees is tantamount to igniting a race war, and that is exactly the opposite of why you were elected.

Undoubtedly, incidents of a racial nature will occur on your watch, and you will be tempted and expected to comment on them. Avoid this instinct. Remain silent on the most intense racial issues. Occasionally you can comment but do so in a more symbolic fashion, perhaps by inviting the aggrieved parties to your home for a beverage, awkward conversation, and photo ops.

Be perfect

Black people in general are under the microscope. Black people who have the power to launch drone strikes in foreign lands are under even more scrutiny. Millions are looking for an excuse to oust you, and making mistakes, no matter how small, gives them ammunition. So do yourself a favor. Use spell-check, floss regularly, know the answers to every problem in the universe, and be perfect. Simple.

Initiate the plan for reparations, white slavery, and radical social and economic transformation

For some segment of White America, you will never be American. You will never be a legitimate president, despite the fact that you've placed a high-definition streaming video loop of your live American birth on the homepage of whitehouse.gov. They are convinced that you are a threat and are waiting for you to come out and publicly reveal your true agenda. Fortunately for you, I've figured out just what that is.

All of the previous advice was about creating the impression that you are not in the White House as an expression of black rage and revenge. That is a feint. You are exactly what your enemies fear. You are about revenge on white Americans. Woohoo!

Now, even with the powerful title of president, you have to

be circumspect in how you initiate the revolution. Declaring martial law and sending troops into white neighborhoods, forcing interracial gay marriages and liberating every single black prisoner would be swift, but would also trigger certain resistance and make our work much more difficult.

No, what you need to do is implement policies that could not possibly be connected to your plans for total race war, policies like even more expanded health-care coverage, radical financial markets reform, and infrastructure projects like high-speed rail. Of course, behind the scenes, each of these is part of your larger plan to destroy White America.

By expanding health-care coverage further, you expose more white Americans to doctors, doctors who can administer drugs, drugs you can contaminate with powerful mind-control compounds that will allow you to hijack the minds of millions of white Americans without suspicion.

By claiming to rein in the out-of-control financial system, what you're really doing is installing backdoor computer systems into the bank accounts of every hardworking, red-blooded white American (blacks will be exempt from the electronic banking Trojan horses). Any white citizen who dares to criticize your policies faces the threat of a highly targeted financial bomb. You can destroy their credit rating, sell off their stock holdings, or trump up evidence that they've purchased child pornography online. Those who escape the mind-control doctors will be hesitant to resist when faced with such digital economic catastrophe.

As a last resort, you will of course be forced to build concentration camps to house members of what remains of the White Resistance. It is an unfortunate necessity, but do not shy away from it. This is why you were really elected, and being president is about making and following through on tough decisions. Besides, you've already installed the banking hacks. Don't back down now. Your economic re-stimulus provided the cover you needed to build the camps under the guise of "construction jobs that cannot be outsourced" (nice job playing to nationalistic instincts, btw), and high-speed rail provides a clean, efficient transportation system to move millions of whites in and out of the camps as the labor farms demand.

PRESIDENTIAL POWER-UPS!

The plan outlined so far will help significantly in your quest to be the second black president, but there's always more you can do. Here are two bonus lessons offering radically different paths to the White House. Both are optional, but I urge you to consider them if you are serious about leading the free world.

Alternate path #1: Be conservative!

Being the "second black president" might not feel special enough for you, but you can still be a first. You can be the nation's First Conservative Black President. Conservatives love to embrace black people so long as it's one at a time. Some of them even voted for Obama in 2008, but they prefer when they can come up with a conservative version all their own.

When Obama was running for the Senate, conservatives threw up Alan Keyes against him. Keyes wasn't particularly qualified and didn't live in Illinois, but he was black! After Obama's inauguration, the Republicans elected one of their five black members, Michael Steele, as chairman of the party, effectively shouting, "We have a black guy, too!" During the 2012 election season, many conservatives were enthralled with Herman Cain, another black dude, whose relevant political experience consists of having run a pizza shop.

As a black person, you would be a dream presidential nominee for the Republican Party. They could claim that they openly support black people, while your policies work to actively undermine that community. Stay open-minded about this path.

Alternate path #2: Be the open revolutionary they fear you to be

As explained earlier in this chapter, much of White America fears a black president because of the idea that he or she will exact some sort of revenge on white people. This fear of the uncertain possibility can cost a black president significant amounts of support and credibility, as President Obama has learned.

As the second black president, you could break from the deceptive path I laid out earlier and choose instead to be upfront about this plan of ours. Why hide your plan under the label "health-care reform" when you can just call it what it is: *My Program for White Enslavement.*

The American people and media have an incredibly short memory despite technological tools that allow for infinite storage and recall. Every election season, some candidate makes a ridiculous assertion that we all forget about in a matter of weeks or even hours. Remember when Rep. Michele Bachmann signed that pledge claiming black kids were better off under the two-parent households of slavery times than today's preponderance of single-mother households? Remember when Texas governor Rick Perry called Federal Reserve chairman Ben Bernanke a traitor and implied he would be killed in Texas? Remember that time when President Obama strangled those three dalmatian puppies to distract from yet another disappointing jobs report? The lesson for you is clear. If you get this issue out in the open early enough in your campaign, by the time people vote, the shock will have worn off and any of your opponents or members of the media who raise the issue of your White Slavery Initiative will look petty and out of touch for bringing up something you've already addressed countless times.

Good luck, Sir or Madam Second Black President, and may God bless these United and White-Enslaving States of America!

How's That Post-Racial Thing Working Out for Ya?

AT ONE point during my writing of this book, someone suggested to me that I title it *Thoughts on Post-Racial America.*
I calmly informed this person that the only way the term "post-
racial" America was getting into the title of my book is if it was
called *Post-Racial America Is Some Bullshit, and Other Thoughts on
How to Be Black.*

It is hard to escape some mention of this concept after 2008.
As damali put it, it's almost as if America is saying, "We're breaking up with you, black people. It didn't work out."

The Black Panel, including its white Canadian member, uni-
versally agreed with me that Post-racial America is indeed some
bullshit:

Christian Lander: We're definitely not post-racial.
W. Kamau Bell: That was always a media creation.
Cheryl Contee: [It] was a fantasy.

damali ayo: That phrase cracked me up!

Elon James White: I can't discuss [it] because it doesn't exist.

Jacquetta Szathmari: [It's] kind of like a unicorn, maybe, or a leprechaun. There's an idea that it exists out there, and some people believe in it, but really, it's not there.

Derrick Ashong: I'm sorry. Post-racial America is bullshit.

The people have spoken! And even though my statistically significant panel was unanimous about the nonexistence and bullshit nature of "Post-racial America," they had different ways of thinking about why that was and what it meant.

Let's hear from the white Canadian (Christian Lander) first:

Obama was supposed to bring about Post-racial America in one election, which is fantastic, if it could happen. I think the reaction since then, just looking at how people react and to the anger people feel, the inability to believe that he is actually an American, just kind of proves we're definitely not post-racial.

The rage people have to [Stuff White People Like] *recognizing differences, just recognizing it's there, is just another signal that* [America] *is not post-racial, and it's a huge problem.*

The idea that some people see post-racial as meaning we don't see race at all, that everyone is exactly the same, there are no cultural differences to anyone anymore, that's even worse. That's just as ignorant and just as terrible.

The harm I see from ignoring racial differences fundamentally comes down to stupidity.

[I], as a white Anglo-Saxon Protestant from Canada, and a first-generation Chinese or a third-generation Chinese person in

Canada—even though we grew up literally three blocks apart, went to the same high school, had all the sort of socioeconomic checkboxes that you would think defined a completely level playing field—we have totally different life experiences. They're not the same at all.

To not recognize that not only is stupid but it also demeans the experience of those other people. I don't think you can ever achieve cultural understanding by pretending that cultural difference doesn't exist.

Both Kamau and damali had direct experiences around Obama's election, guaranteeing they would see Post-racial America as a fantasy.

Kamau:

I remember the night that Barack Obama was elected. I was in San Francisco walking around, and there was a buzz in the city and people were all excited. You just heard people have conversations in the street. I was walking down the street, and I turned a corner, and it was weird. These white people were [excited about the result, yelling,] "Barack Obama!" I turned the corner, and they went, "Oh!" It was this weird thing where they were so excited about that black guy being president but not excited about this black guy right here. It was clear, and they responded as if I caught them saying "nigger" or something. It was just this weird gasp . . . and this is living in San Francisco.

The idea of discussing Post-racial America . . . seems dumb. It's like talking about Reconstruction. That period is over. It's a historical thing that we'll cover. We'll be like, "There was this thing called Post-racial America for two weeks," and then they'll realize, "Oh? No."

damali:

Two weeks before [Obama] was elected, somebody called me the N-word on my street in my neighborhood back in Portland. So, it was really clear that this was not going to happen. But the country has been trying to push black people under the carpet for a while.

The art world went through this phase where they were calling things post-black, which was insanity. I think it's the same thing that is happening with this. If you're not saying, "We're post-race," then we don't really want to hear you, because you're bumming us out. So, it just, it's crazy.

Human beings have this infinite potential for courage that they rarely tap. And if people would just dig down and be genuinely honest with themselves, we would all be living in a much better culture. But instead, we're very much addicted to avoidance and cowardice, I think.

Jacquetta's point seemed to flow naturally from damali's belief that post-racial anything is about avoidance.

I don't understand what post-racial means. Does that mean that I'm not going to be black anymore? Or are they just going to get rid of affirmative action? That's what I thought would happen. When they said post-racial they'd be like, "All right, pull up the ladder. Everything is done. Bootstrap your way through. We're finished. There are no more races anymore. We don't have to help you out, and we don't have to acknowledge that there's any difference between white people and people who aren't white."

That's really the issue, right? It's about white people trying to get rid of race so they don't have to deal with their issues with it. That's

what I thought was post-racial. I don't think any black people think
that there's post-racial unless you went to Oberlin or something.

Meanwhile, Cheryl and Elon acknowledged that the *ideal* of
post-racial may originate from a positive place and not just from a
"cowardly" White America, even if its *reality* eludes us.
Cheryl:

Post-racial was a fantasy. I think it's something that people really
want, I think there's an urge and a healthy aspiration to becoming a
Post-racial America. I would love to see that day. I don't think we
live in that world right now.

Elon:

I understand the idea. I understand that even for black people,
sometimes you just don't want the struggle anymore. You don't want
to discuss struggle, you don't want to discuss oppression, you don't
want to discuss all the dumb shit that has happened for years and
years. You don't want the feeling of burden when you turn on the
television in February. God forbid you go near the History Channel,
and you find out about all the shit that happened to all of your
people! You don't want it. So, the idea of this time when it's all over
is very intoxicating. It's easy.

In a weird way, I would love to argue for it because I wouldn't
have to discuss the dumb shit. But it's also putting your head in the
sand, and it's also not understanding the idea of repercussions and
ripples of events happening in our country. And that's my issue with it.

I don't blame white people for Post-racial America . . . I believe that the idea probably wasn't negative. It was probably this idealized concept, and it probably came from a sense of privilege . . . It never happened. And two years later, after Post-racial America was ushered in, we are more racially tense now than we've been probably in the past twenty years. So, you know, post-racial can suck it.

That's what I'm going to do. I'm going to say things that sound like deep and intelligent, and at the end of it I'm just going to go, "And they can suck it."

I'm going to leave it to Derrick Ashong to close out this assessment of Post-racial America. He agrees with others that it isn't real, but he also sets forth a direction that resonated with me.

America is not now post-racial, and America will likely not be post-racial anytime soon, and America will have a significant problem so long as she is interested in being post-racial as opposed to getting to the point where race is no longer a problem.

People will always find ways to determine who is in and a part of us, and who's an outsider. And part of that is because . . . I define me to some degree in the context of you. I'm not just me existing in the world. I am, in part, me because I'm not you. We are part we because we're not y'all.

So folks will always find ways to create differences. The question is how much do those differences matter?

There was a time in this country when it was a big deal if you were a Catholic. That was a problem. There was a time in this country when it was a big deal if you were a Jew. Problem. Right now in this country, it's a big deal if you're a Muslim. Problem. But, you know, you go down the street, you go in to eat in a little place and you're a Catholic, a Jew, who cares? Everybody's marrying each other, making little brown babies that don't know whether to go to church on Friday, Saturday, Sunday, so they just be at the club.

So basically, it's one of these things where what was a problem ceases to [be] as much of an issue. That is what is also happening with race, and it will continue to happen with race. Now you see a lot of beef right now because people who are used to, and whose worldview has been created in the crucible of how things once were in this country, they hearken to the good old days, which were not necessarily that great, even for them, frankly. But they hearken to those days, they yearn for those days of yore.

They forget that, yes, fifty years before the 1950s they were killing Irish people in New York. Their memory is limited. They forget that, yeah, you might persecute somebody for being Muslim here, but the Puritans who came out here back in the 1600s showed up to escape religious persecution.

So I know that societies and people tend to have a short historical memory, but that history happens anyway. We are moving and we will continue to move to a point where race will not be the primary issue that binds or divides us. We'll find something else, and we'll combat that, too.

So if the future is a United States in which race is no longer the primary issue that binds or divides us, then (a) why have you read this far in a book called *How to Be Black*, and (b) what's the future of blackness in America?

The Future of Blackness

THIS BOOK has been my chance to explore a theme that is essentially personal, necessarily political, and often hilarious: how to be black. Based on what I've learned through the process of putting this book together, I'm going to put forth a plan for the future of blackness in America. This plan is mostly prescriptive in that it's full of ideas that I and those I interviewed want for Black America, but it's also descriptive because it's based on things that are already under way.

The Grand Unified Theory of Blackness consists of three major components.

1. New Black History: teaching a more complete and honest history of black people and, thus, America in far more interesting ways
2. Distributed Struggle: spreading the burden of fighting oppression more broadly across society

3. The Center for Experimental Blackness: opening up the doors of blackness by passionately embracing the eclectic, the nonracial, and whatever else suits your fancy

1. NEW BLACK HISTORY
Say it loud! I'm black and I'm proud!

Let's face it, given most of what is commonly taught as black history and how it's communicated, the subject can be depressing. The quick viewfinder perspective is: snatched from Africa, dragged across the sea in the least accommodating of accommodations, delivered into slavery, stripped of language and religion, freed (reluctantly), terrorized for generations and, generally speaking, treated like crap. My people, this is not an uplifting story. It's a downer.

Derrick spoke to some of the psychological harm that can come from internalizing this image of yourself as a loser, saying, "I think that black [Americans] need to love ourselves more. There's a lot to love, and part of the problem we have is that our history is not adequately taught." He continued:

> *If you look in modern-day history, and the modern world—the West, New World, Africa, the Old Worlds, whatever—and you remove the historical context, it's easy to believe that you're less than. African-Americans make less money; they live shorter life-spans; they have higher health risks; they have lower general economic outcomes and lower expectations. You would think, "Oh, well maybe they are less than, right?"*

He described a girl in Ghana who said to him, "You've got to admit that white people are better than us . . . I mean look at them. They have everything," as well as a group of black Americans who frustratingly asked why more slaves didn't fight back and escape. Both cases represent people who don't know the full story, the history of the compound effects of advantage and white privilege over time as well as the history of never learning the stories of your people who fought and succeeded in breaking out of their circumstances.

But Derrick wasn't the only person to describe this tragedy of an exclusively negative understanding of black history. Elon spoke of it in the context of watching the History Channel during February, and Jacquetta complained that anytime she was told about black history, it was generally along the lines of "Things suck for us!" Accepting such a negative spin on your own history necessarily affects your view of your own self-worth, your potential, and your place in this world, not to mention the view others have of you.

At the same time, I believe we need to make room in these lessons to acknowledge the pain of our upbringing in House America. There are long-term psychological effects of long-term abuse, and the constant dehumanization and attacks on families won't be erased just by telling positive history tales. Those tales need to include the dark side and maybe an American Therapy Program, not just for black people as the victims of abuse but for the entire nation.

The New Black History Course aims to address these massive gaps, and it isn't simply some repackaged Afrocentric curriculum that says, "Black people were kings and queens back in the day, and The White Man is terrible!" Instead, it's just an honest and more complete version of events.

But at the heart of this new education plan is the story of the critical place black people occupy in American history.

America. Fuck yeah.

The United States is a pretty special place, in a good way. Growing up with knowledge of this country's significant imperfections and the cost black people have paid for those errors, I always looked askance at the notion of strong U.S. patriotism. I wasn't prepared to wrap myself in the Stars and Stripes and sing loudly of the land of the free and the home of the brave. I didn't hate America, but let's just say I was skeptical of its awesomeness. I often felt as Frederick Douglass did when he said in his 1852 Fourth of July speech, "I am not included within the pale of this glorious anniversary!"

Of course, there's a difference between his perspective on America and my own. He was an actual former slave. I'm the great-grandson of one. Yet as I look at my own story and that of my family, even as I write this book, I recognize that this is an impressive and bold country whose ideas of what it means to be a country are still, over 230 years after its founding, revolutionary.

The missing link for many inside and outside of Black America has been to fully understand the role black people have played in helping make those beautiful ideas more tangible and more real.

Our early existence in America exposed the nation's shortcomings from the start, and thanks to our struggle, America has become more of what she has the potential to be. As Derrick put it, black people in America "have literally been the physical embodiment, the manifestation of the ideals that the Founding Fathers said they believed in, thought they believed in. But they didn't exist until us. That's something to be proud of."

True black pride is also American pride, and black people truly are the most American of people in this country. We have nowhere else to go! So as much as we might feel some distance between us and the U.S., and as much as others may try to push us away and claim directly or indirectly that we're not "real Americans," that line of thinking is patently false and is a disservice to everyone.

This country is our home, and we helped build it both physically and morally. The struggle of black people in America, therefore, is the struggle of America itself to, as damali put it, "get behind its own dream."

So that's a sampling of what the New Black History Course might consist of: a broader story of the Diaspora with a special focus on the Americanness of black people in America. In addition to what we pass on to each generation, it's also important to change how we teach these lessons. Looking toward other ethnic groups in America may provide a partial model.

Jacquetta elaborates:

[My husband and I] have a lot of friends who are Chinese, Jewish, whatever. On Saturday morning, they get to go up to their ethnicity school and learn about them. We don't have that. They make it fun. They make it exciting. There are games with Hebrew. There are games with Chinese, et cetera.

When I was growing up, people were always like, "You've got to be black. You've got to be black." But they made black sound like it sucked. It was always about getting into trouble or fighting or being oppressed. It was never, "We're going to get together and be black, have some awesome food and tell stories . . ." They never put a face on black that was like, "Yeah! Fun!"

What do we do? I don't know. We complain about it. But why not have a Saturday school program where you can go and learn about us? It doesn't have to be just African-Americans, okay? Anyone can go. But put a nice face on it.

Then, when you turn a certain age, you get to have a ceremony or something, and then you're black! And then no one else could ever take that away from you, no matter what you do. No matter if you go and work for Booz, Allen & Hamilton. Doesn't matter.

I love the concept of a Certificate of Blackness that you'd get upon completing the special Saturday school, but the larger point of making the story of black history more attractive is a point well taken. Once we've got that down, we can free ourselves even further.

2. DISTRIBUTED STRUGGLE

What do we do about today's struggle against racism? Do we need a "national conversation on race," as many mainstream media figures tend to think? No, according to Elon:

I'm not interested in having a national conversation on race. I don't believe a racial conversation can actually happen and be meaningful. I believe that every time this stuff happens you're either preaching to the choir or you're talking to people who don't understand or don't care. The only thing you can do is put out information, and put out as much information as possible. And when people hear the information, they will go back to their own world, and they'll think about it, and they'll figure it out, and that's how it will grow.

That's what the Republicans are doing. They're not having a "national conversation" around conservative ideals. They just keep saying shit, and then eventually people come along with it. The same [is true] with the Tea Party. They just keep talking, and talking, and putting it out there, and then people will go back home and they'll think about it themselves. And then they'll either join your cause or go completely against you, and want you in the street choked, like me. But that's what's going to happen.

So maybe we don't get tens of millions of people to sit around the national table and discuss race. We just start putting our ideas out there, yet how do we actually attack contemporary problems? We do what some of the most successful American businesses do. We outsource and collaborate!

I'm not suggesting we directly ship anti-racist warrior jobs to Indonesia to take advantage of less expensive labor, but the gist of the plan is to spread the costs of Black Struggle Operations across a larger base.

Outsourced struggle?

Certainly part of being black in America is acknowledging "the struggle," but there's got to be more to it than that. Blackness has got to be more than suffering and fighting racism. In 2007 the NAACP held a symbolic funeral for the word "nigger." I don't think this has led to any reduced usage of the word, but the idea inspired me. Since then, I've wanted to hold an actually meaningful ceremony making the destruction of racism the official responsibility of white people. It would be like passing off the Olympic torch. You could literally have a black person holding a flaming baton whose dancing flames spell RACISM, and he or she would hand it to a white person, and then it would be their problem. We could stream it on the Internet!

damali firmly agrees with the core of this proposal.

There's only so much we can say to white people anymore about this, because we've been saying the same things to white people for generations, decades upon decades. It is now really up to them. You're going to learn it or not. You're going to take care of it or not.

I've done workshops where I have literally taken all the people of color out and left the white people and said, "Your job is to end racism, and I'll be back in twenty minutes. You set it up. Take it down."

I like it: shock doctrine for ending racism.

Do you know what would happen to black people if we could hand over responsibility for ending racism to white people? Our high blood pressure would subside. We would live longer. We would smile more! Kamau could do a different one-man show! And for white people, it's a good deal, too. Fighting racism builds character, and makes you a better person.

Let's do this, America!

Collaborative struggle

The program of Distributed Struggle doesn't end with handing the racism baton to White America. Kamau introduced a concept I wish I could take credit for.

Black people get so caught up in the black struggle that we forget to be caught up in other people's struggles. And we forget to realize that we should be just as concerned about their struggles as our struggle. And it's really sort of frustrating me.

Any black person who's not with the people in Arizona, on the side of the immigrants, you're an asshole. Not that it's the same thing, but these are all struggles of oppressed people. Any black person who's like, "Gay marriage???" Let me just sit you down and talk to you for half an hour. I get you think gay is creepy. But other than that, there's no way you should be [opposed].

I've recently come to the conclusion: I think that all people who are fighting for oppressed people should only be allowed to work for the group that's one over from them. Black people should only be allowed to work for the Mexican immigrants' struggle in America. Mexican immigrants should only be allowed to work for gay marriage. Gay marriage should only be allowed to work for black people. I feel like if we all just stepped one group over, I think we would get things done a lot quicker.

You can't end racism and make sexism worse. You can't end racism and make homophobia worse. You have to put it all forward . . . So a big part of my how-to-be-black is actually trying to be inclusive of all the struggles. Slow clap.

Yes, he actually said "slow clap" at the end of his statement. I had to leave it in!

The first two components of the Comprehensive Plan for New Blackness are about clearing items off the runway. A better understanding of our history and a shared sense of responsibility for "The Struggle" should help lighten the burden we often feel as black people in America.

In terms of history, it's worth considering that while black Americans share history with the rest of the Diaspora, we aren't bound by it in the same way as other groups are by their culture's expectations. We are uniquely American, and America is young. Jacquetta compared this to older cultures that might feel threatened by a new thing.

> *It's the Wild, Wild West of African-Americana out there. You don't have to stick to five thousand years of a traditional culture.*
>
> *There are some cultures which are like, "No, that is not Jewish, and that is what we do not do." I have a lot of Jewish friends, and every single one of them have told me that their parents are like, "Jews do not run." So then they don't do sports, because there's five thousand years of a wonderful tradition that they feel like is telling them that. We don't have that. You can do whatever you want.*
>
> *There's no road map for being black.*

So where do we want to go, black people?

3. THE CENTER FOR EXPERIMENTAL BLACKNESS

This is the fun part. I just want you to know that when I started this book, I had no idea it was going to become a program for the Evolution of Blackness, okay? But it is, so pay attention.

One of the most consistent themes in my own experience and those of The Black Panel is this notion of discovering your own blackness by embracing the new, the different, the uncommon, and, simply, yourself.

For Kamau, it was finding an eclectic mix of pop-cultural role models that allowed him to "assemble my own version of blackness."

Growing up, because I didn't feel black the way society told me I was supposed to be black (and I think I was squeezed out by white people and by black people where I grew up), [that] really allowed me to sort of find my own way. In that sense I felt like I've always leaned towards an eclectic way of putting things together . . . I feel like that's one of the strengths of the way that my approach is. I don't feel closed out of things.

For Elon, it was about embracing his passion for putting information into the world.

Black people define blackness with everything we do. So, right now I'm shooting this video and someone's sitting there in their house thinking, "Ah man, black people love shooting videos on green screens," because I'm defining it. People are like, "Why do you have servers in your house?" I'm like, "Because I need information, this is how I put stuff out there." Because black people like computers, son! We love server farms, we like LAN gaming, and we define it every time we do something.

For damali, it was about connecting blackness to themes far beyond race, such as sustainability and eco-living.

Black people can be more than professional black people. I had an eco-friendly clothing company for a while, and I'm really passionate about sustainability issues. These things are not separate.

My role model for the sustainable community is the Sea Island settlers, who were the black people who moved to this island after slavery. Because, of course, what were they really good at? Farming. They set up a community, grew their own food, had their own schools. They were separate. They were a nation unto themselves, and then the government shut them down. It was too threatening.

That is something that black people own, that self-sustained community. That's my history, so it's always connected for me and I get really excited about that.

So be open-minded. We are too young a people to accept the limitations placed on us by some in our own community or especially by those outside of it. As Jacquetta said well, "There's no perk in being closed-minded as a minority. It's never, ever, ever going to help you, ever. It's not your world . . . We're 12 percent. We're a minority, so get off it."

Jacquetta also took this idea of pushing the envelope of blackness even further than being open-minded. She has a program in mind.

If I had a lot of money, you know how Jewish people have birthright? I would give every African-American boy or girl, when they turn sixteen, one year somewhere else, wherever they want to go, to go and experience what it feels like to be black somewhere else.

When I went abroad as an African-American, when I went to Western Europe, when I went to Eastern Europe, and particularly when I was in Hungary, I had people come up to me and go, "Oh, you're American! Are you a teacher or are you dentist or doctor?" I thought I was going to fall on the floor.

*Don't believe what you see here. The way that people want
you to see yourself through the media, and that's pretty much all
you're getting, is not really the way that we are seen everywhere. Go
and meet African Germans, African British people, African Dutch
people, African Chinese people, African African people.*

*Go outside and see what is out there in the world. Do not be
trapped in this incredibly narrow definition.*

One of the challenges emerging in an era of Open Source
Blackness (you like how I keep creating new big labels?) is a grow-
ing gap in the common experiences of the black community itself.
As Jacquetta put it:

*All of a sudden, black people just start doing crazy stuff, like
that guy who was doing speed skating. When did brothers start
doing that? Just crazy. And then they'll want to go to Harvard, and
then they'll want to travel, and then they'll start doing mad stuff.
And then what do we have left there? What will be the common
experience?*

However, that reality exists today. That's part of the point of
this book, right? Being black can be a different set of experiences.
Jacquetta acknowledged this case of "the center not holding" in
her own story.

*My husband is white. He is a Cyprian-American, and we have
more in common than I do with black people I've met who are just
from LA. I just can't understand where they're coming from, because
they are from a different region of the country . . .*

Or people from Chicago, who I don't get. African-Americans from Chicago, they have a whole different way of living that, for me, for a black person from the Eastern Shore of Maryland, it's difficult to bridge that gap. There should be an app for that, I think.

The app would allow African-Americans of different classes, socioeconomic status, and political affiliation to communicate [with] each other without beef, kind of like a Rosetta Stone situation to eliminate beef and misunderstanding.

I hereby dub this app the "Negretta Stone." Yes, I went there. And now you wish you had thought of it. Check your local app store for downloads.

Are you keeping up? We've got experimental blackness abounding at this point, but how do we make it stick? How do we replace the overwhelming media images of limited blackness with a more expansive concept?

It's already happening. You've got the Afro-Punk movement and Black Geeks and the black people who love nature, and more. You look at what people like Elon are doing with media production, and they are getting new ideas, new images, and new expectations out there. It's not enough just to be black in your own way. We also have to tell the broader story of blackness to counter the damage inflicted on us by the narrow tale told by others. That's where Cheryl's vision comes into the picture.

I think that we're living through almost a second Harlem Renaissance. But I would say that the scope of that Renaissance is much bigger than it was in the 1920s, and it's powered by social media, so it can reach a lot more people than it could before. In the

1920s, when you're talking about Harlem or Paris, it was a very small group of intellectuals, artists, poets, singers, dancers that were in conversation with each other, and ultimately it had a ricochet effect over time in the popular culture.

But right now, we're starting to drive that culture in a contemporary way, and in a way that they couldn't before, because they couldn't really reach that many people, given what they had at that time. [But] right now, we've got this thick stew of people in heavy conversation not only with each other, as you saw in the Harlem Renaissance, but with the larger group . . .

That is really exciting for what it means for the future of African-Americans in this country and the cultural impact, the economic impact, the social impact that we can have in a positive way that also is shared with the larger culture.

I think that the people who are coming up behind us are even more literate with these tools, are even faster communicators. We are going to see this amazing uprising in a positive way of African-American thought and music and art that will astonish the world.

Booyah! I can see it, too, and my skin tingles at the thought. In many ways what led me to the people I ultimately interviewed for this book was the faster-than-history communications network we have nowadays. Elon's videos, Cheryl's blog posts, Derrick's music, et cetera. All of these are part of this more global, collaborative resurgence of black culture and thought (what Derrick would call "Afropolitan"), and when it comes from the bottom up like this, it challenges the prevailing and limited images of blackness peddled by our major media but also the limited expectations of many black people themselves.

So, black people, let's repeatedly put out information about our own images of blackness, be it fighting for justice or making videos on a green screen or hosting TV shows on Al Jazeera or camping or writing books about the infinite possibilities for how to be black. As Elon put it: "Don't let someone tell you what you should do because you're black. You do what you want to do, and then you open up the doors of blackness."

As Shakespeare wrote, "There are more ways to be black than are dreamt of in your philosophy."* Dream bigger. Just be, and the blackness will follow.

---

* You should know by now that any time I claim to be quoting Shakespeare, I'm lying.

Race Work and Art—The Black Panel Speaks

I grew up watching and listening to all sorts of comedy, most of which was introduced to me by my mother. On our budget vacations, we would tear through Old Time Radio comedies on the car stereo: *Lum & Abner* and *George Burns & Gracie Allen*; Garrison Keillor's *A Prairie Home Companion*; and stand-up comedy tapes of Bill Cosby, Whoopi Goldberg, and Richard Pryor.

We never had cable television in our home (I didn't get cable until after graduating college), but we loaded up VHS tapes of Eddie Murphy, obviously supported shows like *The Cosby Show* and *A Different World*, and my mom got me into British sitcoms. Thanks to PBS, we could get shows like *One Foot in the Grave*, *Are You Being Served?*, *Keeping Up Appearances*, and my favorite, *Chef!*, which starred a black man as a perfectionist chef whose command of his kitchen was powered by a seemingly inexhaustible fusillade of verbal putdowns.

In high school, I expanded on my own performing life and began doing plays and musicals with social messages. My time at Sidwell Friends was a big part of this experience. Every year I attended, we put on a Black History Month musical review, and out of this experience, I discovered the youth activism and theatre group City at Peace.

My childhood, as designed by my mother, didn't just feature an introduction to comedy and art, but it also introduced me to the concept of art as a communications medium for ideas and even activism. My stand-up comedy has always been political at its core, and even my Web-based performance art pieces have a component of advocacy and social message (I once treated a mayoral contest within the mobile application Foursquare as a real-world political campaign). *How to Be Black* exists very much in line with that tradition, and while I definitely intend for it to be funny, there is a message in it.

Along my own artistic road, I have encountered others similarly engaged, people who tell stories but in a style far more accessible than straightforward lectures. It was from this group that I selected my interview subjects for The Black Panel. I knew that the topic "How to Be Black" was bold, massive, and possibly presumptuous on my part. I recognized that many people could write a book with such a title, and some have and more will. After all, being black is just *being*, right?

So to augment my own limited experiences and voice, I wanted to recruit my comrades in the arts to this mission. In addition to the questions you've seen them answer throughout the book, I asked them directly about their writings, videos, songs, and performances. I wanted to know why they chose that path to say the things they thought needed saying about race and politics in America.

It has always been my goal with this book to shine a spotlight on people who I thought were "doing blackness well," and so in the spirit of show-don't-tell, I want to more fully introduce you to the work of The Black Panel. Let's start with Christian Lander, the white man from Canada.

CHRISTIAN LANDER

The website *Stuff White People Like* swept through America like a sort of political tract. "Have you seen this website?" people would ask. I'd get e-mails from friends and strangers, "Yo, check this out. It's a site about white people!" It was through this word-of-mouth Internetting that I discovered Christian, but when I really gained respect for him was the spring of 2010.

We were both slated to speak on a panel at a conference on Internet culture, called ROFLcon. Our topic was "Race and the Internet." Along with Terese and Serena Wu (purveyors of fine Asian-American family satire sites *My Mom Is a Fob* and *My Dad Is a Fob*), we discussed how we played with race online. Christian and I hit it off big-time, and by the end of the panel, people in the audience were demanding we do a show, any show, together.

For this book, I visited Christian in his Los Angeles apartment. He really does love Asian food and really does live in Koreatown. In his living room, with him seated in front of a map of North America, I asked him how white people had responded to *Stuff White People Like*.

Anything I write about, people are going to be furious about,
and more often than not, it's white people who are angry about it.
They're angrier than anybody about it.

They're angry that "just because I'm white doesn't mean I can't
like this." I'm not saying that, I'm saying you do like it. And so they
sort of contradict themselves a little bit. But they get angry and say
that pointing out that race even exists IS racist. That's their theory.

I don't even know how to react to how angry they are about
saying that recognizing that we're different is racist. No, judging
based on the differences is racist, but recognizing the difference is
there is not racist at all.

Continuing on the theme of people's reactions to *SWPL*, I
wondered if he had heard from non-whites who identified heavily
with the site's listing of all things white. Indeed he had.

People who aren't white come to me all the time after
[completing the test in the back of the Stuff White People Like
book], and they'll go, "Oh, my God, I'm white. I can't believe this!"

Humor was the top priority [for Stuff White People Like*],*
and I never denied that, but there was a message behind it: all of the
things in the list, aside from having black friends and stuff like that,
for the most part (Whole Foods and living by the water, and all this
sort of stuff) they're just things, and anybody can participate in it.

These things are definitely class-based more than anything else,
and it's a class that's overwhelmingly white, no matter how much we
don't want to recognize it. We want to believe that the middle class
is perfectly balanced. It's the perfect mix. No, it's disproportionately
white. Absolutely, without question.

Because Christian's work is explicitly comedic and particularly satirical, I asked him how important satire was to his message.

The role of satire in talking about race is essential. I can't stress enough how important it is. I spent a lot of time in graduate school, and what I found so much in an academic setting is that people are petrified to say the wrong thing.

At the end, nothing emerges, no progress has been made. If people aren't talking, there's no progress.

So if you're talking about any sort of racial issue—it doesn't matter what it is—and you're so scared that you're going to offend the entire room with what you actually believe, you won't say it.

And you won't see that "wait, you're not completely wrong, or you are completely wrong," and you bottle it up and you won't say it.

When you set the room for satire, and you set the room for humor and sort of that ability to say kind of whatever you want, people feel much more comfortable talking about it. I think that that just puts everyone so much more at ease, to actually talk about this idea of cultural difference. And the idea of race and class still being fundamentally tied together.

I know from teaching in grad school for four years that a lot of undergrads are still kind of figuring out things and some of them are very angry at race. They still really see affirmative action as a huge injustice against them, and they have all this pent-up rage that they won't talk about, because they're petrified of being seen as racist.

So when you bring this up in a context of humor, there's so much more comfort, on their side, to talk about it, and to let it out. And then as they're doing that, you can kind of point out:

"Why do you think this list of stuff counts as white?"

"Because most people who consume it are white."

"Well, what do you need to consume it?"

"Well, money."

"There you go!"

And so you lead the horse to water and you let it drink.

I think humor is absolutely essential. When you come at somebody to talk about race, especially if you have an ax to grind as a white person who is angry, or as someone who is not white who is angry, the audience you're speaking to will be petrified. They'll be petrified to say anything. They will agree with whatever you say and nothing has gone forward.

Finally, I wondered what Christian thought of truly hateful people who utter some nonsense but then try to cover it up by saying, "I was only joking! I kid! I kid!"

People trying to hide behind the shield of satire are interesting. For me, who makes a living making fun of race, making fun of white people, it's hard to say what exactly is acceptable and what works and what doesn't. It's like the old ruling on pornography where the judge says I can't define it but I know what it is when I see it.

You don't really have to be that smart to tell when someone's satire is coming from a place of intelligence and not a place of hate. It is so hard to disguise the hate that comes out of people who try to call it funny.

When I started SWPL *with my friend Miles, we always thought it would be funny if people took the idea and went in the right direction with it. So there're sites like* Stuff Black People Like, *written by black people;* Stuff Asians Like, *written by Asians;* Stuff Black People Hate, *which is hilarious. It's sort of done in this way. It's done from the inside, it's done with love, it's not done with hate.*

But people have done all these horrible sites where they'll do Stuff Black People Like with all the old, horrible stereotypes: watermelon, fried chicken, crime, all that sort of stuff. And it's awful.

But there's the difference, right? You see it. I think it's really easy to tell when it's coming from hate and when it's coming from satire.

W. KAMAU BELL

I had heard about Kamau years before I finally met him. People on the West Coast said things like, "He's like the you of the West Coast!" which is actually an odd thing to hear, but I know folks meant it as a compliment. When I finally saw him do his one-man show at the New York Fringe Festival, I was hooked.

When Kamau, Elon James White, and I had brunch together the following day, it was an official bromance. Kamau has been doing stand-up the longest among members of The Black Panel. I wanted to know how he started, and what role race played in his performance.

I feel like the same thing that is in black comedy is in black radio. We call it black radio, but what we really mean is hip-hop and R&B radio, because black radio does not encompass all of black music. I feel the same way about black comedy. That's like R&B and hip-hop comedy, and it's just like a stylistic thing that I don't do.

I can play there but sometimes it's like when they play Lenny

Kravitz on a hip-hop station. Sometimes it's, "That's a refreshing change!" Sometimes it's, "Get this bullshit out of here!"

[I did an audition stand-up set] for Comedy Central. It was a mostly black audience, all black performers, and I went up first or second and I did a joke that referenced Gandhi and everybody just [went silent].

I hate when audiences are purposefully dumb, because I know everybody in the room knows who Gandhi is. And if you don't, that's you. That's not me. That's you. And I hate when audiences do that thing when they come to comedy clubs and they turn their brains off. This is black audiences, white audiences, Latino audiences . . .

There's a thing where audiences just leave their brains outside. So when you say something like Gandhi—I'm not doing anything eloquent about Gandhi; I'm just referencing him as a cultural reference that we all know—you could just see them go, "Nah, we don't do that. We left that outside." And so I got off stage . . . and the MC said, "Give it up for Kamau. You can tell that he reads!"

And he followed it up with, "But I don't!"

And the crowd went, "Ahhhh!!"

I talk about race in my comedy a lot because it was the subject that when I started doing comedy was the most verboten. Especially in Chicago and performing in white rooms, I could talk about anything, but if I talked about race they would tighten up.

I think it was because of the way I talked about race. I wasn't doing it from a "Kings of Comedy" perspective. I've never been a big proponent of "black people do stuff like this, and white people do stuff like this." It usually ends up that the black people do things poorer than white people.

He started really committing to discussing race in his comedy when he considered how much time he is actually on stage.

You only get to be on stage for a very short percentage of your life. If you think about it as far as a job that is being done, people work eight and ten hours a day on their job. If you're on stage an hour, five times a week or seven times a week, you're one of the best in the country at it if you have that much stage time, and that's seven hours a week.

So I feel like you're only on stage a short period of time, you might as well talk about something you care about and you might as well talk about things that you feel you bring something to that nobody else does.

I also asked him about the history of his show.

I have a one-man show called The W. Kamau Bell Curve: Ending Racism in About an Hour. *If you bring a friend of a different race, you get in two for one. It started as a response to the fact that I would go to comedy clubs and talk about race and racism a lot, and I felt like after about twenty minutes people go, "Next subject!" It's not that they even mind the jokes necessarily all the time. But they just sort of, they get fatigued by the subject, which I think is bullshit.*

Especially in this era, I think that's bullshit because you can Google every comedy club you go to before you go there, and look up every performer, and go to their YouTube page and find out if that's the place you need to be.

So I decided I'm going to write the show that I thought I was going to have to wait to be famous to do, and that became The

W. Kamau Bell Curve, *and the whole idea was that I'm going to make sure everybody knows it's about race and racism.*

The title was a joke, obviously, but it would also be great to be able to do. And at the time I thought, "Ending racism in about an hour?" I thought, "Hopefully I'll have an hour of race and racism stuff to discuss."

[The show started out as my] proving to the audience that racism still existed, because this was in October of 2007, when we were, "You know, that Barack Obama guy could be vice president one day if he's lucky, if he's real lucky." It was also on the heels of Michael Richards having the explosion in the comedy club, and Dog the Bounty Hunter, and James Watson, the DNA guy. There were all these, as I call it, "Nigger Tourette's Moments."

Then around the time of Barack starting to run for president, racism sort of came back. It came back like skinny jeans and high-fat ice cream. It became like a thing again.

CHERYL CONTEE

It's taken me years to realize how close Cheryl and I actually are. I first met her via e-mail in the summer of 2006. She had started *Jack & Jill Politics* and was blogging under the name Jill Tubman. A mutual friend had suggested I join as a partner in the role of Jack.

We met in person a few weeks later at a progressive blogger conference now known as Netroots Nation. I decided on the name Jack Turner for my *JJP* persona, and we've been helping drive the *JJP* ship since. It wasn't until a few years later that we realized we had both attended Sidwell Friends, though we just missed being there at the same time.

The incredible ride we experienced on *JJP*, especially during 2008, wasn't anything either of us could anticipate. We started the blog initially as a personal outlet to get tension and thoughts off our chests and minds.

At the time, black people and blogging was kind of a new thing. And if you look at the political blogs in particular from that period, almost all of them were started anonymously or pseudonymously.

In fact, during that time, people would say to me things like, "Gosh, you seem less angry." And it's because all of that fury was channeled to a certain extent [into] the Jill persona.

One of the premises of sites like *Jack & Jill Politics* is to give voice to a new generation of political thought, and criticism of existing black leadership was a big part of what drove Cheryl's blogging in the beginning. I asked her what she thought about black leadership today.

In terms of black leadership today, I think there's also a transition. There's the Civil Rights generation that is starting to age out, frankly. And they are very reluctant to go.

That's part of what Jack & Jill Politics *was all about, was actually pushing back and providing that voice of the hip-hop generation, and talking back to the Civil Rights generation, to the baby boomers, and saying, "Look, we're here. Our opinions matter. And frankly, we've had a different American experience than you. You worked so hard to create that, but now, let us articulate what that actually looks like and how we can build a future based on those experiences."*

Cheryl's vision of a "Second Harlem Renaissance" is one I find to be so powerful. She spoke of it primarily in terms of art and culture, but given her political activities, I also asked if she saw a similar renaissance in black political involvement.

I think where that translates into the political realm is that now if you saw during the Barack Obama candidacy this amazing outpouring of African-Americans who hadn't ever voted before, discovering their political power, again, we're just at the root of that.

The tree has yet to grow in terms of African-American political power in this country and the ability for our ideas and for our values to impact in a positive way the national dialogue on where we want to go as a country.

ELON JAMES WHITE

Elon and I are constantly mistaken for each other within certain left-wing blogger circles, and we love to joke about it because we are, in fact, so very different. We generally acknowledge that he's the angry progressive black comedian, and I'm the happy one.

I first came across Elon after I moved to New York from Boston. He was producing black comedy shows called "Four Shades of Black" that felt nothing like traditional "black comedy shows." There were no jokes about women's feet or black people's credit ratings. Instead, people talked about college, iPods, relationships, and even pterodactyls.* It was a refreshing alternative image.

---

* Comedian and actor Baron Vaughn has a great joke about pterodactyls. You should look it up.

Now Elon is known primarily for his award-winning Web series, *This Week in Blackness*, and the regular Web radio show that accompanies it, *Blacking It Up*.

I asked Elon about the origins of *This Week in Blackness*.

I started This Week in Blackness *in September 2008. Initially, it was a project that was commissioned by VH1. They wanted a black Best Week Ever. And so, I had done something [proving] that my blackness quota was high. So, they were like, "Yeah, could you come up with this idea?"*

Being black in 2008 meant you were probably very political. It's not even that you really wanted to be like, "I want to talk about policy." It was because it was 2008, Barack Obama was running for president, and everyone also already knew who you were voting for, no matter what happened.

WHITE PEOPLE: Oh, so what happened at that debate last night with Obama?

ELON: I don't . . . Why are you asking me? I didn't volunteer that I knew that.

But they would just assume. So, then I started This Week in Blackness.

In all honesty, it was a screen test for this black Best Week Ever, and I just wanted to put it out there, see what the response was.

Given the title of this book, and Elon's track record of putting out shows that challenge the prevailing image of blackness, I asked him how people reacted to the title of his show.

The criticism that I receive from having a show titled This Week in Blackness *is, "How dare you? You decide that you're going to speak for black people and you're race-baiting. You're causing division."*

I laugh at these things because one of the few things that I really put forth first within writing and all this stuff is that no one can define blackness. Not one person, not one entity. So the idea of calling it This Week in Blackness *was always a gag.*

There are episodes where it has nothing to do with black people. I argued the Citizens United *[Supreme Court] verdict.* *That's not a black verdict. That was an American verdict and guess what? Black people are American. I know! It's weird.*

I probably skewed it in a way that people that are familiar with black culture would be more comfortable with or they might understand the references more. But that was it.

But I get that, "Oh, you're speaking for black people." And I go, "No I don't." I did a video called 13 Black Truths *and one was: "No one can speak for black people." And the video clip that was right next to me, it was a sign that popped up that says, "Not even the dude who hosts* This Week in Blackness.*"*

On the question of how he started dealing with race in his stand-up comedy, Elon says:

---

* In *Citizens United v. Federal Election Commission*, the U.S. Supreme Court took the extraordinary step of lifting nearly all restrictions on corporate money flowing into election activities and essentially completed the transfer of power from "the people" to corporations. It's pretty great if you live in Delaware and your last name is Inc.

When I first started stand-up I thought I was going to be that special Negro. You know, the one that was like, "I'm never going to mention race ever. I'm just gonna talk about what I find funny." Then I'd get on stage, and I'd do my set, and people would come [up to me after] and they're like, "Man, do you know you're black? You don't even act like you know you're black. That's amazing." And I took offense to it.

So, I ended up having to deal with it, and going head-on with the whole idea of blackness, and what people perceived of me. People would come to the show and go, "I didn't know black people could say this." And at first I'd be like, "Thank you," and then, "Fuck you."

Finally, I know that Elon has a special place in his heart for BET. I asked him what he thought of the network.

BET can go suck a dick, flat-out. Literally, they're my archnemesis. If I saw Debra Lee in the street we would fight. Actually we wouldn't fight, I would just throw things and then run, because I believe she has the force of darkness behind her, and she would just float and knives would fly at me.

Blackness is very widespread. So all of these things have a role to play, even Black Entertainment Television. Saying that, I feel that when you decide to label yourself as a black entity you then carry a certain responsibility.

When you put out really dumb, ignorant shit and you're labeled [Black Entertainment Television], then you bring down a certain amount of criticism upon yourself. And you can't be surprised.

[Their defense is often,] "Well, it's about money." Then don't

call yourself Black Entertainment Television. Call yourself We
Like Dumb Shit. Or Ignant TV. I'll accept it. If Ignant TV was
nothing but black people I'd be upset, but I'd probably not have the
hatred that I have for BET. It's because they try to have this weird,
"Oh, we're so positive for the black community" idea. You know
what? You can go fuck yourself. You're not positive for the black
community. You were trying to make a dollar by using blackness as
a label for your dollar. And I don't like you for it.

DAMALI AYO

Thanks to the fact that I attended Sidwell Friends, I've been
on the Internet since 1993, before there was even a graphical Web
browser. For all my tech heads reading this, I rocked the Lynx
browser and Pine for e-mail. UNIX text interface, represent!

Anyway, I spent a lot of time online in the decade that followed, and I always prided myself on knowing the latest trends in
technology as well as Web culture. In the mid 2000s, I was living
in Boston and was two years into my stand-up career. I had just
begun to think about how to merge my comedy with my love of
the Internet when I found Rent-A-Negro.com.

I was immediately excited and angry. "Why didn't I think of
that?" I thought. The idea resonated with me at the deepest level. I
knew what it was like to be the black person explaining all things
black to white people, and I loved the idea of getting paid for it
even more. I even briefly contemplated the idea of doing a companion site, Rent-A-Whitey.com, which would be for black people who
needed fair housing loans, taxi-hailing services, and job interview
surrogates.

damali also went to Sidwell (conspiracy?), but again, I didn't find that out until later.* We were introduced in April 2010 by my college classmate and friend Lucia Brawley. (Lucia is Derrick Ashong's partner.) I had to make sure to get one of my Web satire heroes into this book, and the timing was perfect.

I met with damali in her LA apartment and asked her how Rent-A-Negro.com came to be.

Rent-A-Negro.com actually hit the Web in 2003, which is crazy because that was early, early, early Web art days. There was no such thing as a blog even then. There were very few websites just kind of starting to mess around with the Web as a medium. There was a great website about man-meat, where you could buy human meat. It was amazing. It was one of the best pieces of satire I've ever seen. So I was looking at that, and Keith Obadike† had done his selling-his-blackness-on-eBay piece.

So there were a couple of tiny little pieces of race on the Web. Blackpeopleloveus.com was just barely out, and I was really, really stressed out.

I was living in a very white community with a lot of white people who were treating me very much like a professional black person. And I was burned to a crisp.

---

* So I thought it would be fun for you to experience the same time-delayed knowledge acquisition as I did!

† In August 2010, artist Keith Obadike listed on eBay an item whose description read, in part, "This heirloom has been in the possession of the seller for twenty-eight years. Mr. Obadike's Blackness has been used primarily in the United States and its functionality outside of the U.S. cannot be guaranteed. Buyer will receive a certificate of authenticity." After 10 days, Obadike's blackness, which started at a bid of $10, closed at $152.50.

I was on the phone with my mom and I was telling her all this, and she said, "Well, damali, you can't just be everybody's Rent-a-Negro," and I thought, "But if I charged them, I could."

So I decided, what the hell? Let's see if it actually will work. I made this piece and I wanted it to seem as real as possible. And with my artistic intention I had every intention of going out on these performative rentals and taking whatever documentary [footage] I could take and then having it be really a performance piece.

I had like a white escort picked out, this big guy named Chuck. I had the whole thing. But then, I started getting rental requests that were really hateful: people who wanted to gang-rape me, people who wanted to hang me, lynch me. And those came from, from what I could tell, black and white people equally. Then I got one that was very threatening, that had . . . I don't know who would put their phone number on a threatening e-mail, but the phone number was my same area code. And I realized that shit was right around the corner, and I wasn't going anywhere.

So I got all these rental requests for me, and then I got a lot of requests from black people wanting to work for Rent-A-Negro.com, serious requests, and résumés and whatnot. Like serious . . .

Somebody I knew who grew up on my block totally pitched me. Like, "Well, I have all these qualifications and I spent all this time in the military, so I'm really good at being a professional Negro." And I was like, "Wow. I didn't expect this."

damali is an all-around artist, who works in visual art as well as performance. I asked her about the role race plays in her work.

*When I was in college, I always thought I was going to be a
writer. I thought I was going to be the next bell hooks, that was my
aspiration.*

*But then when I discovered visual art and conceptual art, I
realized I could make things that could meet people at a variety of
places on the emotional and intellectual spectrum. So I could just
put it out there and literally walk away. And then they would have
an experience and I could come back and dialogue with them about
it. But I didn't have to be such a therapist.*

*So, I find art to be one of the most powerful forces for social
change.*

Finally, as someone who not only performs but also does full-
on workshops, I asked damali to comment on the fears many
white people have of being called racist.

*It shows our values as a culture when somebody says, "I don't
want to be called a racist." Really what they're saying is, "I want
you to like me. I don't want to not be liked. I want to still be okay
with you." They don't mean, "What I really want is to know and
understand experiences of people of color so I don't sound ignorant."
That would be great.*

*And so, it just shows that, as I always have said, we are operating
at this third-grade level of race relations. And it's that third-grader that
goes, "Please like me, do please like me," versus "Can I understand?"
So, that's how I read it.*

JACQUETTA SZATHMARI

I was introduced to Jacquetta's work by our mutual friend Julia back in 2009. It was one of those repeat recommendations where every time Julia and I interacted, she would ask, "Have you checked out my friend's YouTube yet?" For the longest time, I kept responding, "Not yet, but it's in the queue." (Note how Netflix has us all talking like Brits.)

When I finally did check out Jacquetta's work, I understood my friend's persistence. Here was another black person doing it well, being her authentic self and telling her outlandish story of growing up in a rural community of four hundred families on Maryland's Eastern Shore. I knew I had to interview her.

I asked Jacquetta to explain the origins of her one-woman show.

My show is called That's Funny. You Didn't Sound Black on the Phone. *It's a one-woman show, written and performed by me. It's about three or four stories that I weave together about my experience of considering how to be black and kind of rejecting anyone's idea of black. Because my idea was, "Hey, I'm going to be. No matter what I do. If I eat sushi and dance an Irish jig, that's black, because I'm doing it."*

So it's different stories throughout my life where I've been confronted with trying to be black or not be black enough. At every turn, I've kind of rejected that and moved on just to be myself.

As for the message of the show:

Do whatever it is that you want to do, regardless of who you are and whatever the culture you're in says that you have to be. In

*the end, I decided the best way to be black is to be awesome and not
suck, because what else can you do?*

*Then get on with your life, you know? You don't have to do
anything. How could we not be, how could I not be black? I can't
be anything else. I'm not going to all of a sudden be Chinese. It's not
going to happen.*

On reactions to her show:

*I was surprised [by the reaction to my show]. I originally
thought that I would get picketed by some really small NAACP kind
of anger group. But people of all persuasions, ethnicities, political
backgrounds have come up to me and said, "Thanks for telling my
story." So I think there's a lot more people who feel like [outsiders]
than I had originally thought.*

*I had gay people come up to me and say, "That's exactly what
happened to me." I had Italian-Americans tell me that. I've had Indian-
Americans, all kinds of people have come up. I've had white guys come
up and be like, "That's totally how I felt because I was different from
everyone else in my family." So really it's about being an outsider.*

*I think what they like about my story is that it's a happy ending,
and I feel like a lot of African-American stuff in particular is
depressing. Sorry, it's depressing. At the end of my story I basically go
on to enjoy the rest of my life after the show.*

The other aspect of Jacquetta that intrigued me was her politics. She's a Libertarian. It's not every day you meet a black female
Libertarian comedian and writer, so I had to ask her about any
connection between her blackness and her libertarianism.

I don't know if there's any intersection between the two except that, and this is a generalization, but I think most African-Americans are hardcore capitalists. Cash money! You know, commerce, get paid, get stuff done. That is a capitalist system.

I studied economics briefly when I was at Sarah Lawrence. I decided that was the only thing left and I was like, "Ugh! I'll do it." I had a teacher who was very influential, Charlotte Price. And even though I didn't continue with economics, I continued to read on my own and eventually you come across Adam Smith, and eventually you come across the Cato Institute and the [Ludwig von] Mises Institute . . . and you just start to read.

I came to realize that I'm all about liberty. As long as you're not hurting me, I don't care where you stick it, who you stick it to, and I don't want to subsidize it. Enjoy.

My entire family works for the government and I think that they all went in like everyone did in the sixties with great intentions of doing all this stuff, and they saw that a lot of the programs that they were working on became the new slavery or just weren't really fulfilling [their original mission].

I [was disillusioned] with the [Democratic] social engineering of the sixties and seventies, and I can't be a Republican because I just don't agree with their social engineering from the other side. And so, I was looking for something that allowed for maximum liberty and then I discovered Libertarian Party.

Now, we are not very efficient and we definitely have some crackpots, as everyone does. But right now, that's where I see the most options for people of color, actually, in terms of getting liberty is through the Libertarian Party. For gays, for people of color, for women; liberty. So, that's where I am right now.

DERRICK ASHONG

I've known Derrick since 1995 or 1996. We met during my freshman year at Harvard. He was a junior and big man about campus, heavily involved in black organizations, singing in the gospel choir, Kuumba, and generally being the presence that he is. During my spring semester, I got an e-mail from a non-college e-mail list of black people. I can't quite remember what the list was. It wasn't like an all-black-people-in-America list. It might have been black college students, I'm not sure.

But in this particular e-mail was a casting call for a new Steven Spielberg movie called *Amistad*. They were looking for all kinds of people but especially Africans, so I forwarded that e-mail on to the Harvard African Students Association e-mail list. Derrick received that e-mail, followed up, auditioned, and got a part!

He spun that opportunity into further activities in the entertainment business and now heads the band Soulfège, which describes itself as "Bob Marley meets the Fugees on a street corner in West Africa." In addition to this, he hosts a new social media–powered TV show on Al Jazeera English, called *The Stream*.

Basically, I'm taking credit for all of his success.

I didn't get into a lot of detail with Derrick about his process of fusing art with message, but as I was about to pack up my recording equipment, he offered to read a poem he had written some years earlier. I honestly cannot think of a better way to fully close this book than to print that poem and Derrick's explanation in this final space.

WATER
by Derrick N. Ashong

Water, fresh on the lips of one
Who has known no rivers.
What kiss could be so sweet
As the lingering taste of life?

Mama borned a baby
and she slept in the arms of hope
In her eyes she grew a lady
deftly robed in a cloth sewn centuries ago
with a needle threaded in tears
and guided by notes of a song
spun softly in a soul saddled
by a spirit so strong no noose
was ever long enough to break it.
Some people couldn't take it.
How could this thing with a different skin
sing so loud as to drown the stinking sin
of a nation?
Mama's baby was born post-emancipation
but pre-liberation, and so the song that she wore
within her skin was less a tale of times past
than a calling.
A calling.

Knock, knock, knock, knock, knock
"Who's there?"

It's me. Tell the man I came for my Freedom
It called for me while you were sleeping.
It screamed that the hypocrisy of our fathers was
reeking and it needed to get out of the house.

America the beautiful
Adrift in a reverie of her own making.
Had Freedom locked up so long
we wouldn't recognize her if she were taken
from right beneath the flag.
This dress that she wears
is a song we don't care to sing
We'd rather go carelessly marching into
a war we can never win, for the enemy
Lies within.

Who put the terror in terrorism?
Ask any brother shackled in prison,
whether by the forefather's vision of 3/5ths
of a man, or Supreme Court decision that hands
the American crown to the
prodigal
profligate
prefabricate one.
The heir who cries WAR, when it won't be
his son or daughter left to bleed our dreams
into the flood of the killing fields.
How long will it be before America yields
her thirst for violence to the people's need for Peace?

It is our calling.
I done made my vow to the Lord.
Not the "president."

We wear the song of a slave, because in this
home of the brave it was the hated one
who had the courage to cry Freedom.
We don't just sing Love, we live it.
For in our song strives the spirit that taught
us what it means to be FREE.

A Black tide carried us through the slaughter,
And so today we sing like

Water, soft on the lips of one
Who has known no rivers.
What kiss could be so sweet
As the lingering sound of life?

Derrick explains:

That is a poem that is based on Negro spirituals. It literally
references the titles of a series of Negro spirituals, and a number
of chosen Negro spirituals. And it begins with "Momma borned a
baby." And it talks about this baby, we, these people, who are born of
this nation, the crucible of it.
    I wrote it in 2003. I think it was after the invasion of Iraq. And
it was during the Bush administration. I wanted to point out that
this idea of freedom and liberty that you keep talking all about, the

*people who are here right next to you, whom you so disrespect, are
the ones who actually show what that means.*

*So it speaks of water. Water is a theme that I became very much
aware of when I was in grad school studying the history of black
people in the Americas. Because I was thinking about all of this stuff
with oppressed people, and I was like, "You know what? They're
like water. Like, you can stamp down on them, you can crush them,
you could throw them away, you could do whatever you want. But
somehow, they will always find a way to flow in between, into the
seas of anything you place before them. They will flow through the
good, through the bad, through the ugly, and they can be like Bruce
Lee said, like water, soft and yet hard at the same time."*

*I brought up that metaphor in an academic context, but
academia is very esoteric, and I thought this would be something
that I could present to real people if I put it in an artistic form.*

*So I wrote a muse, a poem that is actually designed to go with a
choir, a choral arrangement of an old Negro spiritual.* So you hear
the spirituals referenced in the poem. You may not know what they
are, but the music in the background is showing what they are and
it's harkening back to those spirits.*

*And because I'm African, we revere our ancestors, and we
believe that the spirits don't go away, they're still with us. And this
was my homage to those people who taught this country what it
means to be free.*

---

* The poem was written to be performed with musical accompaniment based on the
Negro spiritual "Hold On."

Acknowledgments

HERE LIES a list of people, places, and things that have helped realize the book you just read. If you feel you have been omitted, please write your name below in the space provided.

My cofounder at *Jack & Jill Politics*, friend, and generally badass Mamma Jamma Cheryl Contee, with whom the journey of this book began.

Debbie Stier, who spotted me from the crowd, lured me into her publishing lair, and helped me find this book's true voice.

My little big sister Belinda, in whose footsteps I've subconsciously been walking all my life.

Black people and non-black people alike. I love some of you.

The Onion, which truly is America's finest news source and perhaps the world's. My humor has found new heights (and depths) and truths thanks to this legendary cultural institution and its sometimes-merry band of misfits.

Derrick Ashong, damali ayo, W. Kamau Bell, Christian

Lander, Jacquetta Szathmari, and Elon James White, for allowing me to interrogate your blackness. You won't believe what you said!

My editor, Barry Harbaugh, who immediately "got" the book and helped improve it to the point where you might get it, too. Apparently, you can't hand over a pile of photos, scream "I'm black!" and call that a manuscript.

HarperCollins for actually publishing this thing.

My security council for being there always.

Selamawi Asgedom, who was the first in my life to insist I write a book. Please send all complaints to him.

Mieka Pauley, for a life-changing phone call that continues to inspire me.

Brooklyn, for letting me claim you.

My managers, Liz and Meredith, for understanding who I am and what I'm trying to do.

My literary agent, Gary Morris, for having my back.

My CAA agent, Adam Netter. It is so good to have the Borg on your side. You have no idea.

Karla and Zane, for being amazing interns and then abandoning me for "jobs."

The Internet and especially Twitter, for allowing my absurdity to go unchecked.

The Universe, for opening and closing doors when I least expected it and most needed it.

_____

(your name on this line)

About the Author

Baratunde Thurston is the director of digital at *The Onion,* the cofounder of *Jack & Jill Politics*, a stand-up comedian, and a globe-trotting speaker. He was named one of the 100 most influential African-Americans of 2011 by *The Root* and one of the 100 most creative people in business by *Fast Company* magazine. Baratunde resides in Brooklyn and lives on Twitter (@baratunde).